BECOMING AN
INDISPENSABLE EMPLOYEE
IN A DISPOSABLE WORLD

Copies of this book may be ordered
by contacting The Neal Whitten Group at

770-667-0881

or

nwhitten@ix.netcom.com

or

P.O. Box 858, Roswell, GA 30077-0858.

Volume discounts available.

About the Author

Neal Whitten is a speaker, trainer, consultant and author in the areas of both project management and employee development. He has nearly 30 years of front-line project management, software engineering, and human resource experience. During his 23-year career at IBM, he held various management and leadership positions where he managed the development of a variety of software products, including operating systems, business and telecommunications applications and special-purpose programs.

In addition to authoring this book, *Becoming an Indispensable Employee in a Disposable World*, Neal is the author of John Wiley & Sons' best-seller: *Managing Software Development Projects: Formula for Success*, now in its Second Edition. Neal has earned a Bachelor of Science in Electrical Engineering from the University of Florida. He is a member of the Project Management Institute (PMI) and is a certified Project Management Professional (PMP).

Neal is a frequent presenter and keynote speaker at conferences, seminars, workshops, and special events/luncheons/dinners. He has written many articles for professional magazines and makes guest appearances on radio and TV shows.

Neal is President of The Neal Whitten Group. His services include those of project management trouble shooter, performing project reviews, training organizations in the practical application of project management principles, and training all members of a project in the adoption of an effective, productive work culture. Two popular workshops are "Software Project Management: The Fundamentals" and "Becoming an Indispensable Employee," both based on Neal's books.

Neal can be reached at The Neal Whitten Group, P.O. Box 858, Roswell, GA 30077-0858; 770-667-0881; fax: 770-667-0588; E-mail: nwhitten@ix.netcom.com.

BECOMING AN INDISPENSABLE EMPLOYEE IN A DISPOSABLE WORLD

Neal Whitten

PRENTICE HALL
Paramus, New Jersey 07652

Library of Congress Cataloging-in-Publication Data

Whitten, Neal.
    Becoming an indispensable employee in a disposable world/Neal Whitten.
        p.   cm.
    Includes index.
    ISBN 0-13-603812-3
    1. Employee motivation.   2. Commitment (Psychology)   I. Title.
    HF5549.5.M63W52   1995   94-40711
    650.1—dc20   CIP

Printed in the United States of America

10   9   8   7   6   5   4   3   2
10   9   8   7   6   5   4   3   2   1

This publication is designed to provide accurate and authoritative information in regard to the subject matter covered. It is sold with the understanding that the publisher is not engaged in rendering legal, accounting, or other professional service. If legal advice or other expert assistance is required, the services of a competent professional person should be sought.
—*From the Declaration of Principles jointly adopted by a Committee of the American Bar Association and a Committee of Publishers and Associations*

ISBN 0-13-603812-3
ISBN 0-13-082756-8

PRENTICE HALL
Paramus, NJ 07652

A Simon & Schuster Company

Prentice-Hall International (UK) Limited, *London*
Prentice-Hall of Australia Pty. Limited, *Sydney*
Prentice-Hall Canada Inc., *Toronto*
Prentice-Hall Hispanoamericana, S.A., *Mexico*
Prentice-Hall of India Private Limited, *New Delhi*
Prentice-Hall of Japan, Inc., *Tokyo*
Simon & Schuster Asia Pte. Ltd., *Singapore*
Editora Prentice-Hall do Brasil, Ltda., *Rio de Janeiro*

DEDICATION

To my mother, Dorothy Casey, a great friend in all seasons; Barbara, my beloved; and Matt, Jen, and Stephanie, life's special treasures.

CONTENTS

PREFACE

Employees today are increasingly viewed as disposable commodities. As a result, uncertainty and unemployment haunt the work force. The good news is that you can choose to become an indispensable employee in a disposable world. This book is about helping you today to become a survivor in the work force of tomorrow. It is about helping you become and remain indispensable in your current position or any other job you choose to pursue. With the unprecedented challenge of global competition and rapid technological change, many workers face an uncertain future. But as the twenty-first century dawns, I believe there will be tremendous opportunities—perhaps the best opportunities ever—for those who are prepared to survive in the fast-changing workplace.

As an employee, are you ready for the future? Are you up to the opportunities? The challenges? Are you interested in learning how to discover and manifest the great potential that exists within you? This book reveals the six major areas for you to understand and focus on—areas that are critical for survival.

This book is for you if you want to

- Contribute to your company and industry
- Be self-employed
- Run or own a business
- Survive the increasingly demanding work force environment

- Work for someone, either as a professional or as a manager
- Influence your company's workplace culture
- Prosper and realize your dreams

For several years I have given seminars on the subject matter presented in this book, and have found that these topics consistently capture the attention, and often the fascination, of audiences. This is the book I wish I could have had at almost any point throughout my career, preferably in the beginning. The many lessons offered in this book are the result of more than twenty years of service in management and leadership positions. My career has afforded me opportunities to motivate, encourage, counsel, direct, and referee. Further, I have learned the importance of finding a balance between my professional and personal lives. Of course, some of these lessons also came about through my experience as a parent of two active and uniquely different children.

A lot of my own knowledge is the result of personal trial and error: falling on my face, getting up, learning why I fell, and trying again. I continuously questioned my behavior and wondered if and how I should make adjustments. I learned a great deal from observing and listening to others. I don't have to tell you that the real world can be mighty tough on each of us. But there are lessons to learn and behaviors to adopt that can make your work and life much more fulfilling, interesting, and rewarding. This book offers such insight. I hope that your investment in this book will pay for itself many times over. And I hope it will not only enrich your career, but give you encouragement, hope, and guidance in achieving your personal dreams. You are worth it!

–Neal Whitten

ACKNOWLEDGMENTS

The views and opinions expressed in this book are mine alone and do not necessarily represent the opinions and views of any other person or company. However, I am deeply appreciative of the many reviewers and supporters who helped make this a better book than it otherwise would have been. I am fortunate to have had these people, every one of them, share some of themselves with me so that I could gain from their perspectives and aggregate wisdom. They also gave me their time and showed they cared.

I would first like to thank my dear friend Lori Vandegrift for her steadfast support in thoroughly reviewing and critiquing the manuscript and the book proposal. I greatly value her ongoing insight and enthusiasm. I am also especially grateful to the following people for the dedicated, candid, and significant feedback they provided me through their reviews of the manuscript: Tanya Kaptsan, Wendy Miller, Bob Rosenman, Larry Whittington, and Bob Williams.

Finally, I would like to thank the following people for their respective comments, suggestions, and/or support as the manuscript evolved into the book: Jim Claggett, Mary Forlenza, Randy Forlenza, Karen Gelveles, Dennis Kmetz, Bob Mayo, Brian Nolan, Jerrie Stewart, Norb Tennessen, Jeri Traxler, Gene Troskey, and Len Zydel.

INTRODUCTION

Almost every day I encounter people in the work force who exhibit one or more of the following characteristics:

- Low self-esteem
- Lack of accountability for actions
- Uncertainty about how to communicate with peers
- Little understanding of the link between customer satisfaction and job security
- A feeling of powerlessness to change or enhance work-related skills
- Inability to strike a suitable balance between professional and personal life

Most people suffer from these setbacks at one time or another, but there is no reason for any of these conditions to be permanent. I am reminded of a quote by Jean-Paul Sartre:

There's only one sin, and that's failing to believe you have a choice.

Will you be one of the many people who, at middle age or later, stumbles upon the realization that life has not gone according to plan? This book offers ideas and behaviors to help you identify and reach your personal and professional goals. The book is designed to be used as a workbook, with exercises and quizzes embedded in the text. To encourage ongoing personal and professional growth, the book includes an appendix of the exercises found in each chapter. The publisher grants permission for these exercises to be photocopied for repeated use by the reader.

Further, the book aims to raise your awareness of the choices you can make to enrich your career and your personal life, and to achieve a synthesis between them. If you don't like something, change it. After all, whose career and life are we talking about? Yours! Therefore, you are the one that must initiate the change.

It is encouraging to know that regardless of past actions, or inactions, the future begins today. It is never too late to start or alter the journey, but hesitation in committing to a course of action will only waste the precious and limited resource of time.

Don't fall into the trap of assuming that your job will be here ten years, five years, or even one year from now. You must earn your job every day and continue to improve your value as a human resource so that you grow with the demands of your job and your company. And if you should lose your job for any reason, you want to be prepared—and highly marketable—with the skills that will help you find meaningful work and continue to prosper.

This book does not teach you how to get ahead of others. It encourages you to actualize your potential to transcend limitations and realize dreams. Our world is changing faster than many would like. And in these uncertain times, one of the most valuable personal assets is the ability to adapt to change. You can choose to become an indispensable employee in spite of living in a disposable world.

Let's now take a closer look at the major areas discussed in this book. The following sections briefly describe the topics addressed by each chapter.

Chapter 1
The Total Employee: On *and* Off the Job

Before reaching one's potential either on or off the job, it is essential that a person gain a strong sense of confidence and self-esteem. This chapter covers areas of personal growth that will help readers more fully actualize themselves in the workplace and beyond.

Chapter 2
A Cut Above: Personal Accountability on the Job

This chapter espouses the importance of being accountable for one's actions. A simple but powerful concept is advanced: Exert influence on the job in the same way you would if you owned the business.

Chapter 3
In Harmony: Effective Interpersonal Communication

How many times has it been said that an organization's greatest problem is the failure of its members to communicate satisfactorily? This chapter offers advice on how people can learn to get along with one another, and identifies thirteen principles of human behavior that apply to the most common conflicts within an organization.

Chapter 4
Treat Everyone As a Customer: Internal and External Service

Every person who works has at least one customer—either within the workplace, outside of it, or both. Ultimately, individual success revolves around one's ability to understand and satisfy the needs and preferences of these customers.

Chapter 5
Your Menu of Skills: Making the Right Choice

Will your job be there as long as you want it? For virtually everyone, the answer is a resounding NO! This chapter explains how to continuously improve skill value and be ready for a favorable position when opportunity knocks—or when you create opportunity.

Chapter 6
The Juggling Act: Balancing Your Personal and Professional Lives

This chapter examines the synthesis of professional life and personal life and highlights the role of an individual's personal choice in striking a balance between the two.

While each chapter of this book can be read independently of the others, it is suggested that the chapters be read in the order presented. As you might expect, the subject matter of this book can have a greater impact if its messages are regularly revisited. Completion of the exercises found in each chapter will further reinforce the learning. The term "manager" is used throughout the book and is intended to mean the person to whom the reader directly reports. The term as used here is interchangeable with "supervisor," "boss," or even a group of authority figures.

One last thought before proceeding to Chapter 1. Everyone has the ability to achieve far more than they typically do. The main limitations, I believe, are an unwillingness to dream and a lack of perseverance in making those dreams unfold. However, it is conceivable that some of these personal dreams will remain unrealized. Nevertheless, their pursuit can help you grow in many ways, and add a dimension of vitality and contentment to your life that would otherwise not be attainable. I strongly encourage readers not to subscribe to the notion that opportunities and successes are for others and not for them.

A German proverb sums up nicely the message that I want to convey:

> *You have to take life as it happens, but you should try to make it happen the way you want to take it.*

I truly hope this book helps you to fulfill your dreams.

CHAPTER ONE

The Total Employee:
On *and* Off the Job

This book aims to teach you how to become an indispensable employee. But before you even set foot in the workplace, there are measures you can take that will help you become a strong and centered person not only at work but also in other aspects of your life. This chapter focuses on overall personal growth, whereas the following chapters are more specifically oriented toward workplace matters. The following lessons are not new, but they bear repeating. The more self-actualized you are as an individual, the more valuable a human resource you will be to both your employer and your extended community. What's more, *you* will inevitably be more fulfilled in the workplace and beyond.

> **self'-ac'tu•al•i•za'tion**, *n*. the achievement of one's full potential through creativity, independence, spontaneity, and a grasp of the real world.

This chapter examines the behaviors that limit self-actualization, then describes how to overcome these mostly self-imposed limitations. The first section lists commonly held beliefs that are, in fact, fallacies. The remaining sections introduce the major behaviors that prevent people from growing, reaching, learning, and experiencing.

Believe in Yourself

This chapter's goal is to help you feel good about yourself. Its purpose is to encourage your pursuit of those things that are important to you. If you thoughtfully consider the lessons presented in this chapter, you will be more open and receptive to the lessons offered in the chapters that follow. But, even more importantly, if you practice these lessons, you may make discoveries about yourself that can significantly benefit you for the rest of your life.

I believe the greatest problem for most people today is that they do not believe in themselves. They do not believe they have the capacity to succeed, or even deserve to succeed, in accomplishing the endeavors they feel are important. Unfortunately, most people are unwittingly taught to think this way by families, friends, schools, work environments, and other social influences.

The fact that so many people are taught not to believe in themselves does not result from some grand conspiracy by the government, a subversive organization, parents, or teachers. It comes about because that is the way our contemporary culture happens to operate. Almost everyone exhibits some form of self-doubting behavior. Overwhelmingly, people have learned to

- Fear failure
- Fear criticism
- Fear risk taking
- Postpone decision making
- Give up after the first attempt
- Worry about things that haven't happened
- Feel guilty about past events
- Put limits on happiness
- Measure success by material possessions
- Avoid attempts to transform their character or situation

Everyone Excels at Something

You are naturally great at something, probably many things. The negative, destructive behaviors in the list on page 4 may be common, but they are not inescapable. Each person has the capacity to transform his or her life and pursue goals that might once have seemed unattainable. *Everyone* is naturally great at something, and usually great at many things; the trick lies in discovering your talent. And while life provides ample opportunity, many people don't expend the time and energy to make this discovery. What a loss it is to live a lifetime bottled in such a small, confined self-perception—never really experiencing the greatness harbored within.

The information presented in the remainder of this chapter offers nourishment—food for thought—to help dispel these untruths and prevent them from encroaching on the potential of each person to find success and fulfillment in any endeavor.

Don't Fear Failure

Most people are taught early on in life that it is not acceptable to fail—at anything. They learn that it is unacceptable to fail a test in school, to fail at pleasing parents and friends, to fail at catching the touchdown pass, to fail the driver's test, to fail to be hired for a job or earn a promotion, or to fail at pleasing one's children. But there is a vast difference between failing at something and being a failure.

We have all marveled at the athlete who wins an Olympic gold medal, the master painter who creates a priceless work of art, the genetic biologist who discovers the defect-causing gene, the Oscar winner, the Nobel Prize winner, the

True or False?

The following list describes assumptions that are commonly believed or acted out. None are true; not even one. Yet, many people believe these expressions *are* true of their own lives. Review the list and note any behaviors or tendencies you recognize in yourself. Then, right here and now, make a conscious decision to reverse these behaviors and the beliefs that lead to them. In the space marked "Comments," briefly express *why* you believe this statement is true of your life.

Self-images should be based on what   ❑ True   ❑ False
    others think.
Comments:

If there is any chance of being wrong,   ❑ True   ❑ False
    it's best to either delay or avoid
    making a decision.
Comments:

Failure is something to fear.   ❑ True   ❑ False
Comments:

People who fail are failures.   ❑ True   ❑ False
Comments:

Risk taking has little to do with   ❑ True   ❑ False
    achievement.
Comments:

The most wise and effective leaders take only small risks.

❏ True ❏ False

Comments:

Intelligence is more potent than perseverance.

❏ True ❏ False

Comments:

Only the gifted can accomplish exceptional achievements.

❏ True ❏ False

Comments:

Most people's best years are behind them.

❏ True ❏ False

Comments:

There are too few opportunities in life because of the number of people that populate our company, industry, planet, etc.

❏ True ❏ False

Comments:

The future has been written; people are not free to chart a new path.

❏ True ❏ False

Comments:

A person cannot control his or her own thoughts.

❏ True ❏ False

Comments:

Pulitzer Prize winner, and so on. We wouldn't dare think of any of these great achievers as failing, or being failures. Yet, what often escapes us is that each of these champions may have failed many, many times before achieving success. The road to victory in any endeavor is inevitably laden with setbacks.

The gold medal athlete probably lost many early races and suffered injuries. The master painter probably created many imperfect early works of art. The genetic biologist inevitably failed in isolating the defect-causing gene with the first thousand or more attempts. You get the picture. These people would not have gone on to accomplish great things if they had viewed their failures as indications that they were failures themselves. Instead, they grew stronger from each attempt. They realized that they were producing results that offered them opportunities for learning, assessing, growing, and ultimately achieving.

Learn From Mistakes

All great achievers meet with failure along the way. In fact, great achievers learn not only from their own mistakes, but also from those of others. They know that nobody lives long enough to make all the mistakes themselves. They also know that the only real failures are the experiences from which they can't or don't learn something valuable.

The notion of failure need not have a negative connotation. Instead, it can be viewed as a learning opportunity. People should not be penalized for failing; they should be encouraged toward—and rewarded for—achieving.

▌ ▌ ▌ Exercise 1 ▌ ▌ ▌
Stepping Stones

In the space provided, list at least ten things that you can do today that you frequently "failed at" in the process of learning. List anything that comes to mind, whether it happened yesterday or when you were a child. Here are a few examples; riding a bike, skating, typing, driving a car, using chopsticks, playing a musical instrument. Try to include unique skills or characteristics that you have developed over the years in your jobs, hobbies, relationships, etc. Examples of these might include patience, listening skills, public speaking, etc.

When you feel the list is sufficiently complete, consciously recall any pain, embarrassment, or frustration you encountered as you were developing these skills. Also bring to mind those moments of breakthrough you experienced along the way, and remember the sense of pride and accomplishment you felt.

1. _____

2. _____

3. _____

4. _____

5. _____

6. _____

7. _____

8. _____

9. _____

10. _____

▌ ▌ ▌

Failure Is a Necessary Stepping Stone to Achievement

The next time you are confronted with an opportunity, or have a dream, or feel an inner urge to go beyond a previous achievement, remember this: You will inevitably meet with failure along the way; it is a necessary stepping stone to achievement. But when all is said and done, people remember accomplishments far more readily than failures. Most importantly, it doesn't matter what anybody thinks about your stumbles, it only matters what *you* think and how you *choose* to react to the so-called failure.

You have the capacity to learn from your perceived failures and mistakes. Draw encouragement from the countless others who either preceded you throughout history or are today achieving breakthroughs. If they can succeed in their pursuits, why can't you?

What's happening? Are you seeing that the many "failures" you encountered were really mileposts of progress? Are you seeing that the steps backward were sometimes even more important than the steps forward in reaching your ultimate goal? See how valuable these failures have proven?

Most people habitually tell others that it is okay to fail in an endeavor, but they don't take their own advice. Whenever you begin to doubt that your own failures can be viewed as great opportunities, repeat the preceding exercise.

Expect and Accept Criticism

Criticism is something we can avoid easily—
by saying nothing, doing nothing, and being nothing.
Aristotle

Who isn't familiar with criticism? It comes from all sides—from friends, relatives, coworkers, supervisors, and even strangers. While there is little that can be done to prevent criticism from coming your way, there *are* ways of dealing with the experience that can make it a much more positive one. Consider the following lessons.

Expect Criticism

You should come to view criticism as an inevitable part of personal interaction. This does not mean that you should live in fear of criticism, or become defensive; rather, you should learn to distinguish between positive and negative criticism. Further, you can take measures to assimilate the valuable feedback while disregarding that which has no constructive merit. Criticism is going to happen—probably often. If you are prepared for criticism, you are far less likely to be caught off guard and far more likely to remain in control of your emotions when criticized.

Welcome Constructive Criticism

Criticism can be categorized into two types: constructive and destructive. You should welcome constructive criticism, that is, criticism that is well-meaning and intended to be useful. Although it may sting at first, constructive criticism should leave you with the feeling that you have been helped and that you have learned something about yourself and the impact that your actions are having on others. Let's look at some examples of constructive criticism:

- You write and distribute a letter to several people within your organization and one recipient calls to say that you misspelled a word.

- During intermission of your lecture, a person sitting in the back of the room informs you that she is having difficulty hearing you.

- Your boss informs you that an account was lost because you did not follow up on a commitment you had made to the customer.

What should you do? In each case, the criticism has taught you something valuable. You should thank the person for sharing the feedback with you, and commit the information to memory so you can put it to future use.

But what about destructive criticism? Destructive criticism is feedback that may have malicious overtones, or that offers nothing valuable to the recipient that would allow him or her to learn and grow from the experience. Let's look at an example.

During intermission of a lecture you are giving, a member of the audience approaches you and informs you that he can't help but notice that you appear to be of Irish descent. He goes on to say that he doesn't like red hair and also has found that all Irish people have quick tempers and small minds and that he has yet to learn anything substantive from such a person—though he continues to search.

What should you do now? You have several options. One approach might be to acknowledge that you heard the comment and are sorry the person feels the way he does. You could go on to say that you hope, through the presentation and interaction with the audience, to enlighten him such that he might reconsider some of his views. In any case, you suggest that it is okay for the two of you to disagree on this matter and you hope the person, by the end of the presentation, feels he has received something of value from attending.

What just happened? The only value for the speaker is more experience in dealing with destructive criticism. The speaker certainly doesn't want to make a bad situation worse and realizes that his response might avoid a scene. Also, the speaker doesn't want this person's opinion to negatively impact the speaker's own self-image or the remaining presentation. A cautionary note: Although not the case in the last example, feedback that appears destructive is sometimes actually constructive criticism offered by a person who has difficulty expressing his or her thoughts in a tactful and articulate manner. Listen carefully to apparently destructive criticism for any useful, but disguised, information. Consider the following examples.

Handle Criticism Effectively

There will always be people who will disapprove of your behavior or decisions. Even the people very close to you will at times disapprove of your actions. Keep in mind that other people's opinions are just that—opinions. To allow other people's opinions to inhibit or negatively impact thoughts or performance is an admission that what other people think is more important than your self-assessment.

Be confident, but not arrogant. If it is honest, your own self-assessment is more important to your personal and professional growth than the opinion of others. If your own self-esteem relies too heavily on the approval of others, you may be giving them permission to control you. Furthermore, if you don't think highly of yourself, it will be evident in your interpersonal relationships. People are naturally drawn to those who feel good about themselves.

So how do you change the way you deal with criticism? As most behavioralists will tell you, the first step in altering behavior is to recognize the existence of the problem. If you believe that criticism from other people prevents you from fully actualizing yourself, try the following:

Every time you receive criticism, constructive or destructive, ask yourself the following question and respond accordingly:

Can I benefit in any way from the criticism?

If yes, then welcome the opportunity to learn and grow. If appropriate, show appreciation for the input. If you feel the feedback is not beneficial, discard it immediately. Consider responding to the person who advanced the criticism in a firm but positive manner.

Handling criticism effectively requires practice, and lots of it. But then again, you have an opportunity to practice each time you receive criticism! Rather than viewing criticism as an entirely unpleasant experience, you can come to view it as an opportunity to learn, improve yourself, and enhance what you can offer to other people. Criticism is truly a powerful learning aid, if viewed in a positive light.

By the way, it's a two-way street. If you find yourself destructively criticizing others, whether intentionally or not, stop! However, once you have a renewed perspective of criticism, you will probably find yourself offering constructive criticism more often than not. And you will also learn to offer the criticism in a friendly and tactful manner—just as you would like it to be offered to you. The most effective employees and leaders are those who have learned the valuable lessons of both giving and receiving feedback.

Exercise 2 is intended to help you distinguish constructive criticism from destructive criticism and to be able to effectively deal with criticism when it occurs. Although this exercise may seem simple, it is good preparation for the more difficult moments when actual criticism occurs.

After you have completed the exercise below, you may want to follow the same procedure with five of the most uncomfortable incidents of criticism you have experienced. The criticism may have been received today, last year, or when you were a child. The key is to choose five high-impact examples. Then go through the same exercise as with the list on page 17.

The purpose of this exercise extension is to help you deal with any emotional scars incurred from the five incidents and to learn something valuable from them. Obviously, deep-rooted scars may take awhile to heal, but if you subscribe to the lessons in this section, you will find yourself better prepared to deal with painful criticism in the future.

▮ ▮ ▮ **Exercise 2** ▮ ▮ ▮
Constructive and Destructive Criticism

Below try to develop a list of at least five criticisms that you have received in the last few days including those that took place on the telephone or through correspondence. List every remark, no matter how seemingly insignificant. Examine each item and decide whether it is an example of constructive (C) or destructive (D) criticism. If you can learn anything at all of value, mark it as constructive. As you mark each entry, recall how you felt when you received the criticism. Recall the incident and visualize yourself handling the criticism with poise. Then extract any valuable learning offered by the criticism. Repeat for each item in the list.

Examples:

Criticism	Constructive (C)	Destructive (D)
1. Ann said my meeting minutes were late.	✔	
2. Dennis said my memo was too wordy.	✔	
3. Norm gave me a disapproving look when I did not side with him on this issue.		✔

▮ ▮ ▮

Constructive and Destructive Criticism (continued)

Criticism	Constructive (C)	Destructive (D)
1.		
2.		
3.		
4.		
5.		

▌ ▌ ▌

The more you visualize yourself maintaining control of your emotions, and acknowledging the lessons you receive from constructive criticism, the stronger will be your inner resolve to effectively handle criticism of all kinds. Practice this frequently, and it will become an automatic behavior.

Take Risks

My experience leads me to believe that many people, if not most, consider themselves risk takers. Maybe not big risk takers, but risk takers nonetheless. They believe this because they have overcome intimidation or fear in order to pursue some course of action. These actions include

- Flying in an airplane
- Questioning the change that a store clerk returns
- Scheduling a doctor's appointment to have a suspicious-looking mole examined
- Taking a hard-to-start car to a mechanic

While these actions require a certain degree of courage, and involve possible risk, they are actions typically performed in the course of everyday life. The following section discusses a much bolder type of risk taking—the type of risk taking that has the potential to change your life in meaningful ways.

True Risk Taking Can Dramatically Change Your Life

Risks of this type are actions that demonstrate reaching out and transcending the parameters of comfort and complacency. Most people do not take risks of this kind on a regular basis, and many people *never* do. Why do people avoid the bigger risks? The reasons vary depending on the person and the circumstances, but here are some common reasons:

- Fear of failure
- Fear of the unknown
- Fear of change
- A feeling that one will not be able to meet commitments
- A sense of complacency—nothing needs to change
- A belief that one does not deserve the potential rewards
- Unawareness of the opportunity to take a given risk
- A defeatist outlook

Risks offer the potential—but not the promise—for tremendous rewards. These rewards may be material or spiritual but are almost always fulfilling. It is human nature to appreciate more those rewards garnered from risk taking than those that come about in the everyday course of events. There is also something about human nature that urges us to go beyond our present state—to challenge our capacities to the point where true transformation takes place.

Your undiscovered talents may lie in sports, music, art, carpentry, math, people skills, teaching, natural science, gardening, or in virtually any other field. But in order to discover your true capacities, it is necessary to give them an opportunity to reveal themselves.

Here's an example from my own life.

People frequently tell me that I have a seemingly natural and positive way of relating to an audience, a demeanor that draws an audience not only to listen to what I have to say, but also to feel comfortable with my presence. Because I *do* feel at ease in front of an audience, I have come to derive tremendous satisfaction from public speaking. Yet, several years ago, I was unaware of this capacity. I feared speaking to groups of any size. When I finally decided to take the emotional risk and go into public speaking, I made many mistakes—lost a thought from time to time or failed to be articulate. With practice I improved and began to thoroughly enjoy the experience of sharing my ideas with audiences full of strangers. It is a great feeling!

Most people must take risks in order to discover their latent capacities or fully realize those of which they are already aware. In this way, people can access a level of fulfillment that they otherwise might never experience. As the ancient Greek historian Herodotus said, "Great deeds are usually wrought at great risk."

Take Risks to Realize Your Goals

It doesn't matter if your personal dream is to climb Mt. Everest or to ride your bike to work. It takes courage to let go of the familiar, but progress is impossible if you do things the way they have always been done. Dale Carnegie hit the mark when he said,

> *Take a chance! All life is chance.*
> *The man who goes farthest is generally*
> *the one who is willing to do and dare.*
> *The 'sure thing' boat never gets far from shore.*

Can you learn to take risks? Yes! If you are not already comfortable with personal risk taking, then start with small gestures and expand from there. The examples below represent minimal risk but will help familiarize you with the risk-taking habit.

- Challenge an outdated procedure and propose a better way.
- Write and submit a paper for consideration at an industry conference.
- Take the exam to become certified in some important aspect of your profession.
- Volunteer to help a difficult customer.
- Attend a party where you do not know the other guests.
- Contest your property tax increase.
- Submit your views to the editorial section of your local newspaper.
- Show a tear at a tender moment.

Routine Small Risks Lead to Bigger Risks

When you become accustomed to taking risks on a small scale, you will find yourself much more willing to take the higher risks. You may find your interests broaden to areas of life that previously seemed foreign or out of reach. Further, opportunities seem to arrive more frequently.

Reflect on the times in your job or life when you took the greatest risks. These incidents probably resulted in some of your most satisfying and rewarding moments. You may also have learned that a risk doesn't have to succeed to be a valuable endeavor. You grow stronger even when risks don't work out. In fact, the person who has never really failed has probably not taken on much risk.

❙ ❙ ❚ Exercise 3 ❚ ❙ ❙
Determine Your Risk-Taking Style

To understand your risk-taking style, list below several of the risks you have taken in the past year. Include both small and large risks, and state each risk in just a few words. When you have completed your list of at least five risks, assign each action one of the following letters in the column provided: S (small risk), M (medium risk), or L (large risk). Is your level of risk taking what you thought it would be? Ask yourself if you are satisfied with the risks you have undertaken in the past year. If no, why not?

Whether you are satisfied or not, you might find it helpful to go on to the second list, which allows you to identify the risks you would like to pursue in the next six to twelve months. Again identify each risk as S, M, or L. In the last column, identify a specific time or opportunity to carry out the risk. You might, for example, identify one risk that you will pursue each week or month, and another risk that will be taken at tomorrow's staff meeting.

Past Risks	(S)	(M)	(L)
1.			
2.			
3.			
4.			
5.			

❚ ❚ ❚

Determine Your Risk-Taking Style (continued)

Future Risks	(S)	(M)	(L)	When
1.				
2.				
3.				
4.				
5.				

▌ ▌ ▌

You will be pleasantly surprised at the results as you continue to evolve in this area of your life. If you feel the need, you can create a new risk list every six months or so. For some people, this technique increases awareness of the changes they want to bring about and helps them to routinely check their progress.

Take Control of Your Life—Make Decisions

Be willing to make decisions.
Don't fall victim to what I call
the 'ready-aim-aim-aim-aim syndrome.'
You must be willing to fire!
General George S. Patton, Jr.

When people do not make crucial decisions, they surrender decision-making power to others. In effect, they pass control of their life and goals to other people. Much of the behavior that inhibits people from taking risks also prevents them from effectively making decisions. However, the two acts should not be confused with one another. Making a decision always precedes taking a risk; it is the first step to risk taking. By making a decision, a person commits to a certain course of action; the risk is the actual implementation of this action. Let's look at an example: A new project is coming up that offers you the possibility of a lead position. Your manager has assured that you can be assigned to the project but he cannot guarantee that you will move into the lead position. You decide to accept an assignment to the project and lobby for the lead position. By making the decision, you have taken the first step. The risks—such as the possibility that you will not obtain the position, or the possibility that you have overcommitted yourself—will follow.

Make Decisions in a Timely Manner

If you truly believe you do not have sufficient information to decide a matter, then, by all means, seek the information you lack. But it is best to make decisions early—when the potential pain and cost are minimal, yet the long-term impact is most promising. Hindsight will inevitably show that some decisions were not successful. However, if you postpone a decision until virtually no risk remains, you may find yourself passing by the most fruitful opportunities of your life.

> *In any moment of decision,*
> *the best thing you can do is the right thing.*
> *The worst thing you can do is nothing.*
> Theodore Roosevelt

Before leaving this topic, perform exercise 4.

Perseverance Can Transform Dreams Into Reality

> *Nothing in the world can take the place of persistence.*
> *Talent will not; nothing is more common than*
> *unsuccessful men with talent. Genius will not;*
> *unrewarded genius is almost a proverb. Education will not;*
> *the world is full of educated derelicts.*
> *Persistence and determination alone are omnipotent.*
> Calvin Coolidge

All too often, people assume that the success of public figures—athletes, movie stars, authors, musicians, TV personalities, businesspeople, inventors, politicians, etc.—is due to external, fortuitous reasons. People justify the success of these public figures by rationalizing that they were given unique opportunities. These might include

▮ Wealth

▮ Benefactors

Pros and Cons

This exercise describes a technique to help you make a difficult decision. Take a few moments to ponder a decision confronting you. In the space provided, describe the decision in the form of a question. The question should be worded such that it can be answered with either a "yes" or a "no." Now, take either position in answering the question. In the column marked "Pros," write the advantages of this course of action, and in the column marked "Cons," express the disadvantages.

In order to weigh the pros and cons, assign each a value of 3 (high), 2 (medium), or 1 (low), then tabulate the total for each column. If one column has a significantly higher score than the other, your decision should be relatively easy—the higher score prevails. However, if the scores are close, then more thought is required before you make the final decision. In this case, focus mostly on the items to which you assigned a value of three.

Note: If you believe it will be helpful, solicit information from friends, family, and coworkers to help you develop the list of pros and cons. The information you gather may help you see more objectively and realistically the perceived advantages and disadvantages of your decision. The information can also help you test the outcome of making the decision—before it has been made. But remember, the ultimate responsibility for making the decision rests with you; be careful not to empower other people to make decisions *for* you.

▌ ▌ ▌

Pros and Cons (continued)

Decision:			
Pros	1, 2, or 3	Cons	1, 2, or 3
1.			
2.			
3.			
4.			
5.			
Total Value of Pros: _____		Total Value of Cons: _____	

▌ ▌ ▌

- Connections
- Time
- Lack of problems, responsibilities, or handicaps

Occasionally these reasons are valid, but in most cases they are merely excuses people cite to justify their own unwillingness to persevere. If you *want* it, you can almost always *get* it. And a key element of success is persistence.

If You Really Want It, You Can Almost Always Get It

Intellectual and physical capacities vary widely among people. However, it should encourage you to know that perseverance has the power to level the playing field for all of us. People have an innate ability to exercise perseverance and determination in achieving those goals that are important to them. Perseverance can transform dreams into reality. It has happened throughout the adventure of mankind, and it is happening today.

If perseverance plays such a major role in achievement and everyone has the capacity to persevere in the pursuit of their cherished goals, then why are high achievers so few and far between? Why don't more of us play out our dreams? Some of the reasons are listed below.

- Reluctance to commit
- Abandonment of the endeavor after early failures
- Fear of what will be expected once the dream is realized
- Insecurity about one's worthiness to obtain the goal
- Disbelief that the dream is actually attainable

❙ ❙ ❙ Exercise 5 ❙ ❙ ❙
Keep Your Eye on the Goal

In the space below, identify a goal—small or large—that you have avoided pursuing for some time. Perhaps one or more of the inhibitive behaviors listed previously has prevented you from moving forward, or perhaps you have procrastinated for some other reason. It doesn't matter. List at least five reasons why it is important to you to attain this goal. After you have contemplated the reasons, rank them from 1 to 5 in order of their meaningfulness to you and your life. These are the primary catalysts that will help energize you when your perseverance begins to weaken.

Goal:	
Catalysts:	Rank (1-5)
1.	
2.	
3.	
4.	
5.	

❙ ❙ ❙

Everyone's dreams are unique to their experience, and many seem humble in comparison with the achievements of those in the public eye. While perhaps only a few people aim for fame and fortune, *everyone* hopes to achieve something, to be recognized for their contributions, and to make a difference to family, team, department, company, community, or world. As Henry Ford said,

You can't build a reputation on what you are going to do.

Act as if it is impossible to fail, and hang on tenaciously to your dream. Draw strength from each accomplishment, no matter how small it may seem. Perseverance can propel the so-called "common" person to achieve uncommon feats.

After you perform exercise 5, you might like to copy the list onto a separate sheet of paper and keep it close at hand. Put it in your wallet or on your office wall. Make a habit of reading it frequently, especially when your enthusiasm is waning.

Visualize Your Dream Coming True

Much has been written in recent years about the effectiveness of visualization. The technique of visualization can be used by anyone, anywhere, anytime, but it is ideal in a quiet setting. With your eyes closed, visualize starting, progressing toward, and arriving at the moment when your dream has turned into reality. Picture as much detail as your imagination will allow as you proceed along the journey and finally reach your goal. Feel the anxiety and the thrill of reaching your goal. Feel the sense of accomplishment and pride as you visualize your dream coming true.

Here is a personal example.

One of my dreams was to write a book. The day I committed to writing my first book, I came home from work, had dinner, and tended to family related matters as usual. Then I went into my bedroom, crossed both feet up on the corner of my desk, leaned back in my chair, and closed my eyes. I then began to visualize the pursuit and realization of my goal. I had not yet started writing my book and did not have a publisher in mind. But I saw myself going through the thought process of laying out the organization of the book. I saw myself concentrating on the development of a sample chapter, occasionally rewriting and restructuring. I saw myself grabbing hours here and there from my work and responsibilities as a single parent to concentrate on producing the book. Still visualizing, I followed my progress on the book until I saw myself coming home from work one day and gathering the mail from the mailbox. There was a small package about the size of a book. In my vision, I brought the package into my bedroom, sat down at my desk, and opened it. Inside the package was the first printed copy of my book with a beautiful glossy cover. I was elated and excited; my heart pounded with pride.

Almost two and a half years later, after more than 2,000 hours of personal commitment to writing the book, that scene was replayed—exactly as I had visualized it. I came home from work, found a package in my mail, took it to my bedroom and sat down at my desk. I put my feet up, crossed my arms, and for a moment before opening the package, I replayed in my mind the last two and a half years. I then opened my eyes and opened the package. The perseverance had paid off! I had written a book while holding down a full-time job, raising two teenagers, and managing to accomplish whatever else in life was needed to "survive." I had achieved one of my dreams!

Focus on One Aspect at a Time

You must understand that your dream will not become a reality overnight. It will require a lot of perseverance. Although you always want to keep in mind the big picture and the final achievement, it helps to focus on only a single segment of the journey at a time. If you are writing a book, focus on one chapter, section, or paragraph at a time. If you aspire to be an Olympic gold medalist in the 100-meter dash, focus on shaving a fraction of a second off your best time. When that has been accomplished, focus on shaving off the next fraction of a second. If you want to earn a college degree, work toward the degree one semester, one class, one test, or one homework assignment at a time. When you set your goals this way, you allow yourself the celebration of small successes along the way. In turn, this will inspire you to continue.

Set Short-Term Goals

Another tip: Set short-term goals for yourself. That is, if you are writing a book, you might want the first draft of a chapter completed in thirty days, two sections of the chapter roughed out per week. If improving your running speed, you want to shave off .05 second by this time next month. Short-term goals help you to pace yourself. Write down the goals and record your progress regularly throughout a given period of time, for example, every thirty days. In setting these goals and tracking your progress against them, you accomplish the necessary task of challenging yourself on a regular basis. You can do it!

Be Happy

Everything you need to be totally fulfilled you already have.
Dr. Wayne W. Dyer

To be happy, you don't need

- A new job
- A new boss
- A salary increase
- A vacation
- A new car
- A new house
- A thinner body
- Plastic surgery
- The sun to shine
- Retirement

Granted, these boons would be welcome, but none of them are essential to your inner peace or happiness.

Remember, happiness doesn't depend upon who you are or what you have; it depends solely upon what you think.
Dale Carnegie

Happiness is a state of mind, an attitude. It does not come from achieving or acquiring something. When people depend on external factors to determine their relative happiness, they relinquish the power of self-actualization and control of their own state of mind. At best, an external event or stimulus gives people temporary joy; true happiness is a state of contentment *regardless* of outer circumstances—fluctuations of the economy, career instability, social upheavals, and everything else.

Wealth does not ensure happiness, and neither does age, education, or nationality.

If happiness is allegedly free and within the reach of everyone, why are so many people chronically unhappy? Why do they *choose* to be unhappy? Below are a few possible explanations; do you recognize any of these tendencies in yourself?

- Belief that happiness results from the acquisition of material goods, or from the ability to control external events
- Preoccupation with worry or guilt
- A defeatist attitude
- Belief that happiness is a matter of luck
- Unwillingness to change thought patterns
- A feeling that one does not *deserve* to be happy

However you define success for yourself, you will significantly improve the likelihood of attaining your goals if you recognize and exercise your ability to become and remain happy.

Don't Worry About the Future

Many philosophers will tell you that you should not worry. I fully agree with them. There are two types of external phenomena: those you control and those you cannot. If you cannot control the outcome of an event, there is no value, and no potential payoff, in worrying about it. The energy expended in worrying is wasted and irretrievable.

Eliminate Worry From Your Life

But what about those circumstances that you can control? Is it beneficial to worry about their outcome? The answer is still "no." If you have control over the outcome of an event, then put your energy into constructively doing whatever is necessary to help ensure the outcome matches your desires. Let's look at an example.

When I decided to write this book, I did not worry about how well the book would be received after it was published. There were two reasons I did not worry. The first reason was I knew that I had control over the actual text that was written and published. Therefore, I put my energies into planning, writing, rewriting, and polishing the book's content.

The second reason I did not worry was that I knew I had no control over how well the book would be received by each of its readers. I hoped the book would be viewed as a positive influence in helping people to enhance their value both as employees and as human beings. However, each reader must decide the book's worth for himself or herself.

Here is another personal example.

During a seminar I gave on leadership and project management in Sweden, a member of the audience asked me how an effective leader handles worry. I answered the question and provided several supporting examples. From the back of the room a skeptic inquired: "Are you saying that you never worry?"

I said, "Actually, I do occasionally worry. But usually for one minute or less—not an hour, a day, a week, or a year. Sometimes a thought or event will trigger my old habit of worrying and, when it does, I make a forceful effort to channel my energies more constructively."

The skeptic countered, "Okay. Picture this. You are flying back to the States and you are midway over the Atlantic Ocean. The pilot comes on the speaker and announces he is sorry to say that power is being lost in all engines, so prepare to crash into the Atlantic. Now would you worry?"

The audience was sharply alert, eager to hear my reply. I paused a few seconds, then said, "Well, almost no one really knows what they would do in an actual emergency. But I can tell you what I would not do: I would not write a note to those I love. Why? Two reasons. The first reason is that there is only the most remote likelihood that the note will survive the crash and find its way to my loved ones. The second reason is that the people I love already know that I love them. The wrong time to say 'I love you' is at the end. You want to say and express those feelings throughout the duration of your relationships, not just when the end is near. But what I hope I would do is prepare for the crash and either give comfort to anyone nearby that might need it, or enjoy the ride down."

I paused for a few seconds and then added, "After all, it's a once-in-a-lifetime experience."

This example is extreme because it is life-threatening, and most of the things people worry about are relatively minor. However, the concept can be applied to everyday worries. Worrying is a complete waste of time and energy and robs people of the opportunity to enjoy life at any given moment. Channel your full energies into constructive and productive use of your time and let go of your concern about those things you cannot control. I assure you it is a very liberating experience! Learn to eliminate guilt from your life as well. Whereas worry is anxiety about the future, guilt is anxiety about the past—and both are equally destructive emotions.

Eliminate All Guilt From Your Life

In earlier sections, you learned that the future has not yet been created, that you do in fact have the power to influence it. The past, however, is irretrievable; it cannot be changed. So how can you justify feeling guilty about it?

You might want to read the previous paragraph again. This is a difficult truth for many people to accept. Many people are comfortable with guilt. Although people do not have the power to change events in the past, they can attempt to alter the effects of those events. For example, if you have done something you regret, you can attempt to make retribution. At the very least, you can apologize. While I strongly advocate that people take responsibility for their actions, I encourage them also to immediately disregard unpleasant experiences. Do not feel that guilt is a valuable or healthy reaction. Consider this example:

You feel pressured to improve upon your past work performance, and arrive at the office an hour early to prepare for a meeting with an important client. Just before the meeting you argue with a colleague over another account. Frustrated, you make some inappropriate comments and abruptly walk away. Throughout your meeting, you are distracted by thoughts of the earlier altercation.

The point? Many people have a tendency to become easily distracted by guilt and worry. In turn, the anxiety immobilizes them and consumes their mental and emotional energy. Though breaking this pattern of behavior may be difficult, it is absolutely essential to a person's personal growth and well-being.

Some people say that worry and guilt are "natural" emotions, but I believe they are learned (probably early in life). They may seem second nature, but that is only because the behaviors have been with us for so long that they have become very familiar reactions—at least for humans. Imagine a polar bear waking up in the morning to discover his fishing hole has frozen overnight. Do you think the bear's first reaction is to worry about where his next fish will come from or to feel guilty that he did not do his fishing last night before the freeze? Of course not; the bear's energies are focused instinctively on solutions, not emotional obstacles.

Let's return to the notion of happiness. Staying happy means staying in control. It doesn't mean you have to like how events have unfolded. But you recognize the difference between those things that you can influence and those things that you cannot. You channel your energy constructively.

Let's look at an example.

I was addressing a class of high school seniors and discussing the states of happiness and worry. A senior, working hard at wanting to believe what I was sharing, commented, "But if you have a friend dying in the hospital and it is only a matter of days or hours before he will die, it is only caring to worry about your friend. And you should be unhappy at a time like this."

My reply was "There is a big difference between worrying and caring. If you are certain your friend's death is imminent, worrying will not change anything. But caring is warranted and welcomed. Worrying is akin to 'hand-wringing'; caring, however, is an active gesture of giving comfort to another person—a demonstration of compassion and warmth.

"As for being unhappy at this moment," I said, "this is truly an unwelcome, undesirable situation. You care for your friend and wish you had the power to reverse the tragedy, but you don't. You realistically understand this fact and choose to accept it. But happiness is a state of mind, not merely an emotion. Therefore, you can remain happy—that is content, secure, peaceful—even while experiencing deep and painful emotions."

A preoccupation with the past or worry over the future only serves to chip away at your quest for happiness. As Dr. Wayne W. Dyer, author of *You'll See It When You Believe It*, says, "Don't strive to be happy. Be happy!"

The purpose of the following exercise is to offer a new perspective on those situations in your life that you believe inhibit your happiness. The first step in solving any problem is understanding that a problem exists. Once you realize that

Obstacles to Happiness

In the space provided, list several things that you believe detract from or limit your happiness. Be totally honest with yourself. You can list people, events, situations, or anything else, but try to be specific. Write "My colleague constantly complains about my work" rather than "my colleague."

When the list is complete, examine each entry carefully and plot it on the matrix according to whether the obstacle is controllable or uncontrollable, and whether it represents an internal belief or an external situation. Consider these three examples:

1. I don't deserve to be happy (C, I)
2. I am consistently passed over for promotions (C, E)
3. I am losing my hair (U, E)

Items in quadrants 1 and 2 represent situations that you can change. Example 1 is an internal belief that can be (and should be) reversed. Example 2 can also be reversed. The person should investigate the reasons that he or she is consistently passed over for promotions, and take measures to address them. Example 3 represents an uncontrollable, external situation. As such, it cannot be reversed. It is futile to worry about items in quadrant 3; your energies are best spent accepting the situation and learning how to live with it. If you have plotted anything in quadrant 4, think again. There are *no* internal feelings or beliefs that you do not have the power to control.

▮ ▮ ▮

Obstacles to Happiness (continued)

	Controllable	Uncontrollable
Internal	1.	4.
External	2.	3.

▌ ▌ ▌

you control your own mental and emotional well-being, you will naturally begin to be more proactive in establishing (not *seeking*) happiness and prosperity.

I won't tell you that the transformation is easy, or that it can be accomplished overnight. Old habits of thinking die hard. But a sincere, determined, and continual effort to transcend these limitations will *usually* succeed.

You Mirror Your Self-Expectations

Do you believe that success is in the cards for other people, but not for you? Do you find that you often *expect* to fail? If these questions hit uncomfortably close to your beliefs about yourself, then you are right—you won't achieve. You are using a philosophy that I want to better acquaint you with—you are what you perceive yourself to be—but you are using it *against* yourself rather than *for* yourself.

> *If you think you can or you think you can't,*
> *either way you are right.*
>
> Henry Ford

The good news is you can break away from this mold and transform yourself and your life into virtually anything you choose. You might recall studies of schoolchildren that drive home this point.

A group of students are confronted with a new environment (a new teacher and a new class subject) and most importantly, a predefined expectation of their abilities. The students are arbitrarily divided into two groups: superior performers and poor performers. They are told which group they "belong" to and are then treated accordingly. In almost all cases, the students in the superior group perform outstandingly. The students in the poor-performing group perform poorly. These results occur in spite of how individuals performed previously.

Although the human mind is far more complex and marvelous than a computer, it operates in much the same way. A computer performs according to how it is programmed. The information it receives is processed according to the preprogrammed instructions. One unique characteristic of human beings is they can choose to change the way they think. They have the ability to reprogram themselves. Everyone exercises this ability in small ways. Let's look at an example.

A person is suspected of a crime. He is arrested and taken to trial. You have the opportunity to sit through the trial as a bystander. Before the trial begins, a preprogrammed part of you might assume that the person is guilty because of some bias that you harbor. The bias could have to do with the race, socioeconomic background, gender, age, or educational level of the accused. Or perhaps you believe that the person is probably guilty or else he wouldn't have been accused in the first place.

As the trial proceeds, information is made available about the case. Through a series of witnesses, evidence, and data on the accused, you begin to change your views. When the trial is over, the jury brings in a verdict of not guilty, just as you had concluded.

What happened? Your preprogrammed biases were overtaken by information—new data—that you allowed yourself to consider and accept. In effect, you overwrote some of your programming. You might never view the same situation the same way again. As I said, everyone exercises the ability to reprogram themselves in small ways. However, they are also able to exercise their reprogramming on the more important areas of their lives—if they choose to.

Reprogram Yourself to Change Negative Thoughts

Your self-image is being programmed every moment of your life. You, and only you, are the gatekeeper of your thoughts, and these thoughts become the foundation of your self-image. All too often, people take the negative and destructive opinions of others and accept those thoughts as fact. Have you ever asked yourself why you are so quick to believe in others, but so hesitant to believe in yourself? Take control of your thoughts and accept those that fit the image you choose for yourself. Do not let others choose it for you. As Denis Waitley, author of *Seeds of Greatness: The Ten Best-Kept Secrets of Total Success,* says, "...our minds can't tell the difference between real experience and one that is vividly and repeatedly imagined." Consider this example: You and an old friend are reminiscing about your past shared experiences. Your friend describes in detail an event that was special to both of you. But you remember the event differently. When you attempt to set the record straight, your friend suggests your memory is fading. Is one of you lying? Probably not. People tend to remember "facts" differently.

> *Assume a virtue though you have it not—knowing that*
> *the dynamic habit of habit can build it into your character.*
> Shakespeare

Further, the human mind has the capacity to reprogram itself. Everything begins with thought and is controlled by thought. The only limits that exist are the ones people choose to accept for themselves. Most people want to believe in themselves—they want to believe they are capable of taking risks, dealing with criticism, enduring failures, making decisions, and, most of all, feeling good about themselves. While everyone has the capacity to believe in themselves, most people must first *unlearn* the multitude of negative, self-defeating thought patterns and behaviors that have been created throughout their lives.

Read the sentence below, first silently and then out loud. Read it again and again. Repeat it until you feel your resistance and doubt weaken. Now close your eyes and repeat the sentence from memory.

I believe in myself;
I deserve to be what I choose to be.

These are the same words that great leaders and great achievers have echoed to themselves for centuries. Virtually none of their great accomplishments would have come to fruition if they did not believe in these words.

Practice Feeling Good About Yourself

Obtain several small sheets of paper and write on each sheet "I believe in myself; I deserve to be what I choose to be." Then post these sheets in conspicuous places in your home and workstation. Here are a few suggestions:

- Bathroom mirror
- Refrigerator
- Front door
- Car dashboard
- Computer terminal
- Phone
- Datebook
- Television
- Scale

Be creative. If you are uncomfortable making a public display of this affirmation, then you might choose to write the sentence in some sort of code, or substitute a symbol such as a red dot or a particular sticker—anything that will trigger you to repeat the affirmation to yourself again and again and again. As Earl Nightingale said, "You are what you think about all day long."

Opportunities Are Abundant

There is no scarcity of opportunities, only a scarcity of resolve to take advantage of them. You can learn to deal successfully with the behaviors discussed in this chapter, regardless of your age, sex, race, educational level, financial status, or anything else. You are free to choose your own journey. If you think small, your accomplishments will be small. If you think big, so too will be your accomplishments.

If one advances confidently in the direction of his dreams and endeavors to live the life which he has imagined, he will meet with a success unexpected in common hours.

Henry David Thoreau

CHAPTER TWO

A Cut Above:
Personal Accountability on the Job

Chapter 1 showed you how to take responsibility for becoming the person you want to be. This chapter aims to teach you to use many of these same skills to become accountable for your performance in the workplace. Ultimately this characteristic supports the success of both the employee and the enterprise.

Be Accountable for Your Performance

As you perform your job each day, you are confronted with many decisions and choices. You will find that you will be able to make these choices with more confidence and consistency if you apply this simple but powerful concept: Behave as you would if you owned the business.

When people work for someone else, they often lose the sense of personal ownership and responsibility for the outcome of their actions. Whether you work in a company of 5, 500, or 5,000 employees, it is essential that you not lose your identity as an individual and an important employee. Therefore, you must learn to make decisions with the conviction that your personal contributions make a difference. Think about some actions that you have made lately and ask yourself, "If I owned the company would my actions have been different?" For many people, the answer is often "yes." In fact, the larger the company, the more frequently people tell me that they would have acted differently if they owned the business.

Think about it this way: If you *were* the owner, wouldn't you want your employees to make choices as if they owned the business?

You Must Earn Your Job Every Day

Employment is not guaranteed. Don't assume your job will be there as long as you show up for work. You must work to earn your position every day. As George Crane so aptly put it, "There is no future in any job. The future lies in the man who holds the job."

As you read the following sections, keep in mind the concept of acting as if you owned the business. Not only will this perspective help you become a more valuable employee, but it can also make your job more fun and more satisfying for you.

Many of the behaviors in the *True or False* exercise on pages 54-56 have become synonymous with the actions of the "good" employee. But you don't need me to tell you that today's working world is unlike that of the preceding decades. In fact, the climate today is unprecedented. Every week there are reports of downsizing, rightsizing, and other trends that while perhaps necessary are foreboding for employees in all fields. If you want to become an indispensable employee, you must be willing to change your thinking as radically and quickly as the work environment itself is evolving. There is nothing inherently wrong with any of the statements in the *True or False* exercise; in fact many of them represent sage advice for playing it safe. But *no* employee is safe from job loss or job dissatisfaction. The best you can do is to become as valuable, as indispensable, as possible. And that means standing out, being exceptional.

Set Goals

Does the following conversation sound familiar?

Coworker 1: So, what are your goals in the organization?

Coworker 2: Oh, I'm not really certain. I would like to take on more responsibility and eventually receive a promotion.

Coworker 1: Well, do you feel like you are heading in the right direction?

Coworker 2: That's a hard question. I am certainly keeping busy, but I'm not really doing anything unique or definitive to aim myself in a certain direction. I figure I will know what I want to do when I see it. You know, when it crosses my path.

Coworker 1: Have you seen it?

Coworker 2: I don't think so; nothing has turned me on a whole lot.

Coworker 1: It sounds like you don't have any long-term goals within the organization.

Coworker 2: Yeah, but I'm still working on it.

Coworker 1: Do you have any short-term goals?

Coworker 2: Yes, to meet my current commitments and be recognized for doing a good job at whatever I do, hopefully in a manner that will not only allow me to keep my job but also maybe get a salary increase.

Establish Job-Related Goals

If you have established job-related goals and this scenario doesn't apply to you, I applaud you. Unfortunately, however, this scenario applies to a great number of people. It is okay not to know what you want to be or where you are headed

True or False?

Like the *True or False* exercise in Chapter 1, the list below describes beliefs that are all false and potentially detrimental to your career and your company. Yet many people continue to subscribe to these beliefs and act accordingly. Review the list and in the columns at right mark any of the items that you recognize in yourself.

You cannot "empower" yourself;
   a superior must empower you.
   ❏ True ❏ False
Comments:

Always go along with the decisions of
   your team.
   ❏ True ❏ False
Comments:

Never disclose a problem if you can't
   offer a solution.
   ❏ True ❏ False
Comments:

To-do lists create inflexibility.
   ❏ True ❏ False
Comments:

Don't question long-standing
    procedures.

❏ True   ❏ False

Comments:

Avoid measuring processes; they
    add to overhead costs and slow
    down performance.

❏ True   ❏ False

Comments:

Only poor performers encounter major
    setbacks.

❏ True   ❏ False

Comments:

Small, ongoing improvements are not
    as effective as occasional larger
    improvements.

❏ True   ❏ False

Comments:

Don't bother higher management to
    resolve a problem in the lower ranks.

❏ True   ❏ False

Comments:

True or False? (continued)

Never trust your instincts in business. ❏ True ❏ False

Comments:

Most people are not able to initiate ❏ True ❏ False
  important change in their
  organizations.
Comments:

Never bend the rules. ❏ True ❏ False

Comments:

Never exceed your authority. ❏ True ❏ False

Comments:

in your job. But, don't be surprised, or blame others, if you never quite "get there." You must have personal goals in your job if you expect to achieve extraordinary results.

Why do so many people fail to set goals or work purposefully toward goals? Let's look at a few commonly cited reasons:

- I am too busy to look beyond my current assignment.
- Whatever comes along will probably be fine.
- People naturally progress to the next level; no goals are required.
- There is too much competition, so why bother to set goals only to be disappointed?
- I am getting too old.
- My manager will look out for me.

Take the Initiative

If your reason for not establishing job goals is that you do not want any added responsibility, beware! Why? Because the likelihood is high that you must continue to take on more responsibility if you expect to keep your job. In order to remain competitive and survive, employers constantly increase the standards of acceptable performance. You don't have to aspire to become the CEO, or even the department head, but you do need to continuously bring more to your job than you did in years past.

If you are relying on your boss to look out for you, don't! Managers have many people working for them and have their own share of responsibilities. They have problems and pressures coming from their subordinates, peers, and superiors.

This leaves little time for a boss to spend mapping a road to success for each employee. There are rare exceptions, but most people do not work for these exceptions. If you are concerned about your future then you must believe it is *your* responsibility to take the initiative in seeking out opportunities.

Goals help to keep people focused, motivated, and efficient. Subsequently, people have a better chance of remaining competitive—and employed. How should you go about setting goals? Talk to your immediate manager; he or she will be able to share some insights and give information that will allow you to make intelligent choices. Then get another perspective from the head of the organization. Talk to people who currently hold a job that you are considering. Talk to people within the organization whose opinions you value. Talk to family members if your goals can have a potential impact on them. Finally, talk to yourself—and listen!

Choose Goals That Are Important to You

The last item—*talk to yourself*—is the most important. Be honest with yourself and choose goals that are important to you, not to someone else. Remember, your personal effort and sacrifices are what will be engaged in the pursuit of these goals.

Create a Vision of What You Expect to Become

Once you have decided where you want to go in your company and what you want to do, the next step is to create a vision for yourself. Visualize yourself making the decisions and performing the tasks involved in your desired role. With the vision firmly planted in your mind, describe it verbally, and then in writing, in one or two simple sentences. Write the vision in the present tense. Following are a few examples:

1. "I am a successful project manager who builds the most profitable products in the company. My organization consistently has the highest morale and highest productivity of any such organization in the industry. The most significant industry breakthroughs come from my organization." (Junior Engineer)

2. "I am the general manager for the most successful supermarket among hundreds in the same chain. More 'firsts' are piloted in my store than in any other." (Assistant Manager, Produce Department)

3. "I am a wing commander and the pilot of a state-of-the-art attack aircraft that is part of an elite rapid deployment group." (Newly commissioned Second Lieutenant)

4. "I am a full professor at a prestigious university and am a recognized author of a best-selling book on family economics. I am in high demand as a speaker and consultant worldwide." (Undergraduate Economics Student)

After you have written your vision, display it somewhere where you will read it several times each day. You are now ready to list the goals that will help guide you to the realization of your vision. These goals should include time frames and milestones by which to measure your progress. List the promotions or lateral career moves that you hope to achieve in the next two to five years. Finally, make your goals known to those around you. This knowledge will allow them to assist you when appropriate and may inspire them to perceive you in a new light.

It Is Okay to Revise Your Goals

You have the right to adjust your goals at any point along your journey. In fact, I recommend revisiting your goals every six months to decide if these goals are still desirable and whether or not they need adjustment. Chapter 5 discusses more about the classes, training, and experiences you may want to consider as part of your vision.

A word of caution: It is possible that you may never reach the ultimate goal or goals you set for yourself. Even the best of intentions and determination cannot guarantee success in all cases. So it is necessary to not only pursue your goals with zeal but also to enjoy the journey toward them. In retrospect, you will find that even if your goals remain unrealized, you have amassed a wealth of knowledge, experience, and accomplishments.

Manage Your Time

There is generally a direct relationship between how well a person manages the investment of their time and how successful that person is in achieving their dreams, goals, and day-to-day commitments. Denis Waitley, in his book *The Joy of Working,* said it very nicely:

> *Time is an equal opportunity employer. Each human being has exactly the same number of hours and minutes every day. Rich people can't buy more hours. Scientists can't invent new minutes. And you can't save time to spend it on another day...Success depends upon using it wisely–by planning and setting priorities.*

Virtually everyone can improve their time management. With practice, many people might discover as much as several additional hours each day to redirect toward something new or something that has been neglected. Several hours a day is a lot of time to invest in pursuing those things that you perceive as important. If by managing your time wisely you found an additional two hours per workday, you would in turn find about 500 hours per year—more than twelve 40-hour weeks! You can accomplish an awful lot if you were to discover twelve weeks of time spread throughout a year. Through careful time management of an 8-hour workday, most people can readily obtain at least one **extra** hour of productive time.

To-Do Lists

It is important that you spend most of your time working on the most important things. An oft-quoted rule is that of "80/20." This rule states that you should spend 80 percent of your time on the 20 percent of your workload that is most important. The following steps will help you identify and manage your most important activities.

If you adopt this simple technique, you can markedly improve not only your time-management skills, but also your capacity and reputation for meeting commitments. It doesn't take long to develop the list or to reference it each day, but doing so gives you confidence that you will not forget an item. Time management builds discipline into your busy day and allows you to feel a welcome sense of accomplishment as items are completed and crossed off the list.

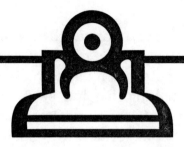

Manage your activities with a daily to-do list.

1. Develop a list of all the things you need or want to do. Attempt to list each item on a single line. For most people, the list will be from a half page to three pages long. Include everything you can think of on the list, regardless of whether it must be completed tomorrow or six months from now. It will be helpful if the list is maintained on a computer so you can easily add and delete entries.

2. As one of your last activities to perform at the end of each week, create a new "mini-list" to contain only the activities that you must accomplish, or begin, the following week. If using a computer, make sure you don't delete the original list because you will be working from the original list each week.

3. With the list of only the coming week's activities, designate the day that you plan to work on each activity. Just to the left of each item, mark M, T, W, Th, F, Sa, or Sun to designate the day of the week. This technique helps you to make certain that activities receive the attention they need when they need it. Another aid is to actually schedule the relevant activities in your weekly calendar.

4. Each morning throughout the week, review the items that must be performed that day. Make sure you accomplish the most important items first. Many people tend to tackle the least important items first because they are done quickly and provide instant gratification. Keep in mind that it is usually better to be late on three low-priority items than on one high-priority item. Of course, the goal is to complete *all* items on time. As an item is completed, mark a line through it.

5. Throughout each week, probably each day, new items will surface that you will need to add to your week's list. Add these items at the end of the list and mark the day of the week that the item must be addressed. If the item applies to some future week then place a unique mark next to it, say an "L" for "later," that means it needs to be worked sometime later than this week.

6. At the end of the week, return to the second step. However, update the original list by deleting the items that have been completed and adding any new items.

Time Management Tips

This section lists tips that can help you manage your time. None of these tips are profound or necessarily original, but they have worked well for me and for others who have adopted them.

Focus on a Single Task

When you start an activity, do not jump to another activity until the first activity is completed. Obviously, if the first activity requires many days, you have to, at some point, spend time on other important matters. However, make every attempt to comply with this tip. Each time you set an activity aside before it is completed, you lose productivity by dragging it back out and getting your mind back "up to speed."

Procrastinate

Procrastinate? You bet! This can be a powerful time saver. Complete activities just before they are due—with a contingency plan built in for the unexpected. If you find that you are more creative and productive when you do things under pressure, this technique is for you. In the late 1950s C. Northcote Parkinson, a British historian and author, coined Parkinson's Law, which states that work expands to fill the time available for the completion of it. I find that many people spend more time working on an activity if they have the extra time to spend. Therefore, they are less productive overall.

Employ a Quick-Retrieve File System

File information in your work environment in a simple, easy-to-retrieve manner. This measure allows you to save time hunting for the material. Keep at hand any reference material or manuals that you consult regularly. Post a list of frequently called phone numbers where you can immediately retrieve them. Your work environment should be arranged for productivity first, appearance last.

Discard Unnecessary Materials and Files

Don't be a pack rat. If you don't need it, discard it. If in doubt, decide whether the item is accessible elsewhere (e.g., library, secretary, coworker, etc.) and if so, toss it. If not, then keep the item rather than suffer anxiety over losing it. The absence of clutter helps you concentrate on the activity at hand.

Plan Trips to Accomplish Multiple Purposes

When you leave your immediate work environment, attempt to make the best use of the trip. Take one trip, rather than several, to visit the restroom, pick up messages, retrieve your mail, and meet with a peer.

Review Mail Only Once per Day

Set aside a block of time each day to review your mail, preferably soon after the mail arrives. This allows you to quickly react if something is urgent enough to require immediate action. If you work in an environment where you can access your mail more than once per day, resist the urge.

Create Three Stacks of Mail

Open your mail and divide it into three stacks:

1. **Essential.** Mail that you must review and act on. Each item in this stack should be added to your to-do list with an indication of when it must be handled.

2. **Interesting but not essential**. Mail that you have some interest in reading, such as magazines and solicitations. Items in this stack should be reviewed after higher priority items have been completed, or whenever you need a break.

3. **Unnecessary**. This mail can go directly to the recycling bin.

Return Phone Calls During a Designated Period

Set aside a block of time near the end of the day—but not after normal working hours—to return your telephone calls. If meetings or planned events throughout the day finish early, and you find you have an extra 10-15 minutes, use this time to return telephone calls as well.

Close Your Door

If you have an office with a door and need to concentrate on a project, leave your door open about six inches. This sends a message to your coworkers that you are too busy to be interrupted for unimportant things, but are available to address urgent matters. If you want no interruptions at all, close the door completely and post a note on the outside. In most work environments, this should only be used as a last resort.

Create a List of Time-Saving Tips

Every work environment has a unique culture, and you probably have a few time-management tips of your own that are specific to your environment. Add your own ideas to those suggested here and create a list to review periodically. Share the list and invite others to add their ideas.

Be Empowered

In recent years, the term "empowerment" has become a business buzzword, but the concept remains underused. Briefly stated, empowerment means understanding one's job, taking ownership of one's job, and doing whatever is necessary (within legal and ethical parameters) to accomplish the job. Many managers and executives cite reluctancy to embrace empowerment as a reason for dwindling revenues and profits. This assertion may or may not be true, but what does seem true is the hesitation of many companies to formally train their employees in the definition and implementation of empowerment. Interestingly, many people find it difficult to fully practice empowerment.

When was the last time your manager reprimanded you for exceeding your authority? If you can recall an incident in recent memory, I applaud you. Many people can't recall it happening to them in the recent *or* distant past. If you haven't in some way caused management to pause and take note of your actions in getting a job done, you probably have not fully embraced empowerment.

Most people tend to play it too safe. They do not stretch themselves to create opportunities for themselves and for their company. If your team or organization were an independent small business and you were the owner, how would you want the employees to act in order to make the business competitive and successful? You would want them to exercise empowerment.

Let's look at some measures you can take to increase your empowerment.

1. **Understand your job.**

   This means meeting with your manager to gain a greater understanding of your job and interface with peers. You must understand your job before you can truly succeed at it. As you embrace empowerment, anticipate the support you can expect from your manager.

   Understand where your manager draws the line between empowerment and insubordination. This judgment is often subjective, so don't assume you know how your manager feels. This dialogue can strengthen the relationship between you and your manager and will likely garner more support than you would otherwise have received.

2. **Take more responsibility for technical and business decisions.**

   I believe that virtually all technical decisions and most business decisions should be made by nonmanagers. Managers are responsible for creating and supporting a productive, safe work environment and for guiding the organization into the future. However, nonmanagers should be given the opportunity, responsibility, and accountability for making things happen—that is, for creating and implementing the day-to-day tasks that move the business forward.

3. **Take ownership of your own personal development and career.**

   You might think it is your manager's responsibility to develop your career. It isn't! Your manager can offer guidance and help you find time to improve your skills and your worth to the company, but it is your responsibility to make this happen. Take the initiative.

4. **Believe that you can make a difference.**

   If you don't believe you can make a difference, you won't. Empowerment shifts the responsibility and accountability to the people who can best make it all happen: you and your peers, no matter what your position in the organization's hierarchy. Consider the following "empowerment" story.

I was asked to moderate a one-day post-project review. The purpose of this review was to discuss what went well and what didn't go well on a particular project. The objective was to learn from both the good and bad experiences and incorporate the learning into planning of subsequent projects. No managers were permitted to attend this review, in order that the team members would feel at ease about identifying the problems. During the day-long review, more than one hundred problems were identified. The view of the team was that more than 85 percent of the problems were the fault of management. During the following week, I spent another full day with the team, this time with the managers in attendance. We discussed the hundred problems and the notion of empowerment. By the end of the day, the opinion of the team was that 85 percent of the problems were not management's fault, but rather the responsibility of various team members who should have taken full ownership of their assigned activities.

What an experience for the team. What a reversal of opinions. Once the team was introduced to the concept of empowerment and the importance of taking ownership and becoming accountable for one's own actions, their eyes opened like never before. Perform exercise 7 now.

Meet Commitments

Many people are quick to make commitments, but slow to meet them. Often a commitment simply translates, "I'll try" or "We'll see what happens." With this attitude, what usually happens is that the commitment is *not* met.

Make Only Good Commitments

If paychecks were based on employees' performance in meeting the commitments they made at the start of the pay period, making commitments and meeting commitments would be synonymous. Why are commitments so important? They are the backbone of business: Commitments are made to customers to deliver products and services, to executives to produce revenue and profits, to banks to service debts, and to employees to pay salaries and benefits. The most popular and successful companies of the future will be those companies that can consistently make and keep their commitments in all areas. And the most valuable employees will be those whose commitments are made selectively and met consistently.

Empowerment and Solutions

In the space provided, list the problems currently confronting you—problems that inhibit the progress of your job. Then examine each entry and decide if the problem is really yours—not someone else's—and, if so, how you might resolve it. Keep the notion of empowerment in mind as you brainstorm possible solutions for each situation. For now, be as creative as possible with your ideas; you can go back later and decide the feasibility and appropriateness of each potential solution.

Problem	Possible Solutions
1.	
2.	
3.	
4.	
5.	

█ █ █

Say "No" Professionally

If you believe you cannot meet a commitment, it is *your* responsibility not to make it. This means you may have to say no to your team leader, your supervisor, your manager, or your coworkers. However, as a responsible employee and professional, you should also offer alternative recommendations. Consider the following conversation I had with a senior planner concerned about making a commitment:

Planner:	I just left my director's office. He requested that I plan the development of a new product and have it ready for delivery in twelve months.
Me:	Fine. Why are you concerned?
Planner:	Because it will take eighteen months.
Me:	How do you know that?
Planner:	I've been building these products for over twenty-five years. I can estimate them pretty accurately.
Me:	I believe you; so what are you going to do?
Planner:	I am going to put a twelve-month plan together and commit to it.
Me:	Why do that if you know that it will take eighteen months to build?
Planner:	Because I can read an organization chart. He's the boss. You act as if you would take a different approach.
Me:	I would. The approach you are considering means you will be a hero for one day—the day that you provide and commit to a twelve-month schedule. But what about the seventeen months and twenty-nine days thereafter, when your plan

begins to fall apart? Everyone who is associated with your plan will be putting in heavy overtime to try and get back on schedule. Product development and manufacturing shortcuts will be taken in an attempt to make the twelve-month schedule. Ultimately, the schedule will slip to eighteen months, at the least. Unfortunately, the quality of the product will also suffer. When you deliver the product in eighteen months—with lower quality than if you had originally planned for eighteen months—everyone will lose: the director who committed to his bosses, the customers who expected something earlier and of higher quality, and all the members of the development and manufacturing team who paid with their personal overtime on evenings and weekends.

Planner: So what would you do?

Me: I would tell my director "no" to the twelve-month schedule. However, as a professional, I would take responsibility for understanding what's driving the twelve-month schedule requirement. I would then develop a list of alternative recommendations. One recommendation might be building a product with less function that could be delivered in fourteen months. It's possible to have a director who has little business sense and can't bring himself to accept anything other than what he asked for. In this case, I might be unpopular for a day. But as the coming thirteen months and twenty-nine days pass, I look better and so does the entire team, the director, and the customers. The next time the director wants a job planned, he will almost certainly come to me because I say what I will do and do what I say.

Make Your Own Commitments

If you are asked to meet a deadline and are unable to satisfy both your existing commitments and the new one, don't accept the new commitment. For example, your boss wants you to commit to a project that will take one week and will be due in two weeks, but you already have a full plate of commitments. It is your responsibility to say that you cannot take on new work without resetting your existing commitments. Most managers will delegate work—it is their job to do so—until the employee says "hold it." Remember, it is *your* responsibility, not your boss's, to manage your commitments successfully.

Include a Contingency Plan

Every commitment should be met. For schedule-related commitments, this is usually possible only if you have built in some contingency for the unexpected, because eventually the unexpected *will* occur. You will find yourself in meetings that you had not planned to attend, your car won't start, you will be out of work with the flu, you will be required to attend a class, and so on. The time contingency you need varies greatly, but as a general rule estimate the time required to perform the task, and add 10 percent to 20 percent more time.

▎ ▎ ▓ Exercise 8 ▓ ▎ ▎
Control Your Commitments

In the space provided, list all the commitments you have made that are still outstanding. It doesn't matter if they are ongoing or are already overdue. In the columns next to each entry, indicate the date you made the commitment and the date you plan to fulfill the commitment. Now look at the list and decide for yourself if your commitments are under control, that is, are they achievable and within reason?

Commitment	Date Made	Date to Be Fulfilled

▓ ▓ ▓

By the way, commitments are not risk free. Depending on the type of commitment, some degree of risk taking is necessary to stretch a person or organization to gain the greatest productivity, for the lowest cost and the shortest schedule. For example, if you are building a product that must compete for market share in a highly competitive industry, it is essential to include some risk in the schedule in order to maximize response to market.

Don't Commit Blindly

Often you will be called on to make an estimate without fully understanding what is being asked of you. Estimates are good business. However, estimates should not be considered commitments. Commit only when you know what you are committing to. In those exceptional cases when you must commit to your estimate, insist on an appropriate buffer contingency. Make only commitments that you believe you can meet. It might be okay to say "I'll try," provided the person you are speaking to understands the risk behind these words. But when you say "I commit," train others to know that this means you can be counted on to make it happen. Then make it happen.

Many people feel pressured by their commitments. If you are not in control of your commitments, there are numerous ways to address the situation. Following is a simple method that allows you to fulfill your commitments, yet gradually gain some control: From this day on, do not make any new commitments until you are comfortable that you can meet them and they will fit in with your work or lifestyle. What does this mean? It means question what is being asked of you or what you are getting yourself into.

Perhaps you want to negotiate terms or compromise or think about it. You have probably heard the saying: "We never find time to do it right, but always find time to do it over." Take control of your time and your commitments. You will gain the respect of your peers, your superiors, your customers, and yourself.

Accept or Solve Problems, But Don't Complain

There are three basic choices you face when confronted with a problem that you perceive is not owned by you. You can complain about the problem, accept the problem with no intention of solving it, or solve it. Let's examine these choices. When a person discusses a problem and shows no intent to constructively resolve the problem, he or she is only complaining. Complaining does not solve anything. Instead, it consumes time and energy that could be directed toward something constructive.

Be Solution-Oriented

When a person identifies the problem directly to its perceived owner, he or she takes a step toward solving the problem and is not merely complaining. The objective is to not waste time and energy discussing a problem unless the discussion is part of the problem-solving process.

In some cases, the best thing to do is accept the problem and learn to live with it. Surprised I would say this? Remember that there are, in effect, an infinite number of problems, but only a limited amount of time available to solve them.

Cautiously select the problems you decide to fix. This measure should be reserved for problems that are especially important to you or your job. An important problem is one that meets one or more of the following conditions:

- Your job performance will be evaluated based on the resolution of the problem.
- You were directed by a superior to solve the problem.
- You have a special personal interest in solving the problem.

Offer Solutions

It is easy to complain about problems that we perceive belong to someone else, and we are often able and willing to name the person responsible. When identifying a problem, try to offer a solution or a set of alternative solutions. Although this is not a requirement, it helps to establish good working relationships among the members of an organization. It also helps to expedite the resolution of problems. Avoid beginning a sentence with any of the following phrases:

- Why doesn't somebody...
- This is really stupid.
- When are we ever going to...
- Why do we always...
- He (or she) doesn't even...
- Can you believe this? Here we go again.
- For a change, I would like to see...

- How do you expect...
- Where did this person come from?

Concentrate on High-Impact Problem Solving

The aim of Exercise 9 is to help you become more aware of your choices when confronting a problem. If you are not pleased with the choices you have been making, you can alter your behavior so that you become more productive with your time and more constructive in working to improve your team or organization. Aim to dedicate most of your time to pursuits that have value to your company, not necessarily to finding problems.

Drive Critical Problems to Closure

I have been requested many times to come into an organization and assess the progress being made on a project. In every case, the top problem I identify is that the most critical problems are not receiving the attention they need in order to be resolved. I am talking about problems that, if not solved quickly, have the capacity to cause significant damage, such as schedules being missed, quality being compromised, costs being overrun, and customers being lost. One might ask, "If these critical problems have such a significant impact on an organization's success, why aren't we better at wrestling these problems to closure?" Let's look at some reasons:

- Fear of conflict
- Fear of "burning bridges" with coworkers

- Uncertainty about what is acceptable behavior in the organization
- Reluctance to make someone else look bad
- Apathy

What causes a problem to become a critical problem, often referred to as an "issue"? When two involved parties are unable to agree on the resolution of a problem that, if left unresolved, has the potential to significantly impact the organization's success, there is an issue. What can be done when an issue arises? If the two parties have made an earnest but unsuccessful attempt to negotiate a resolution, higher levels of management must be called upon to help resolve the issue. This is called an "escalation." Typically, the following rules of escalation should be observed:

1. Escalate only after an earnest attempt has been made to resolve the issue.
2. The dissenter (the person raising the objection) is responsible for escalating the issue.
3. Initiate an escalation within two workdays of knowing the problem is unresolvable.
4. Escalate the problem, not the person. In the rare cases where the issue actually is the person's behavior, proceed cautiously with the escalation. Do not make the issue visible to the public.
5. Always inform your manager prior to initiating an escalation.
6. Always inform involved parties before beginning an escalation.

❙ ❚ ❚ Exercise 9 ❚ ❚ ❙
Problem-Solving Options

In the space provided, list the problems that you have complained about over the past several days. Then examine the list for the entries that actually resulted in some valuable change being made. Next, for each entry, ask yourself if it is worth your time and your manager's time to have you work at solving the problem.

Problem or Complaint	Did It Change?	Is It Worth It?

❚ ❚ ❚

Escalation Is a Healthy and Essential Form of Doing Business

"Escalate" is not a dirty word. The more an organization understands this, the more effectively it can operate. Escalations provide a checks-and-balances mechanism for organizations and help to resolve problems early. Further, they encourage employee participation and ownership of problems. In turn, escalations act to alleviate frustration among organization members and help to prioritize work activities.

There are different approaches to conducting an escalation. For example, some organizations insist that the next levels of management on both sides of an issue be present. Others allow the dissenter to address the issue with the chain of management of the other party, with the optional presence of the dissenter's management. Be certain that you understand the approach taken in your organization. Be mature, prudent, and professional about escalating. Remember, after the issue is resolved, you must go back to work with the person or organization on the other side of the issue. When two parties do not agree on the resolution of an issue, usually neither party is categorically "wrong." Both parties are usually correct from their own points of view and missions. Often a person with broader responsibility for the project is required to resolve the issue and is able to weigh the options more objectively with respect to the overall impact to the project.

After an issue is resolved, both parties should abide by the decision made. Only if significant new information becomes available that could reverse the decision should the escalation be revisited. In every other case, the issue should be considered closed.

Improve Continuously

If it isn't broken, improve it anyway. In today's fast-paced, highly competitive world, it is no longer enough to merely produce a winning product or service. You must also continuously improve, or your competitors—many of whom did not even exist a few years ago—will overtake you. This is the business world of today and it will likely continue into the foreseeable future. You can adapt or you can be replaced.

What is the key to continuous improvement? Learn from what you presently do and apply the learning to what you do in the future. Following are several steps to help incorporate continuous improvement into your own job:

1. Understand how you perform your work today, that is, the process you follow.
2. Measure key aspects of your process.
3. Analyze how you can improve your process.
4. Make adjustments to improve your process.
5. Repeat these steps beginning with Step 1.

Let's examine these steps in some detail. To understand how you perform your work today, you must first document the process and procedures you follow. This documentation can be as simple as a one-page diagram showing the steps you follow in any given aspect of your job. Begin with examination of one aspect of your job, and then another, and eventually pull them all together with one diagram. If this is the first time you have performed this exercise for the process you have chosen to examine, you are likely to discover several steps that can be eliminated or merged with other steps. When you are ready, ask some of your peers to review your process and offer any further insights that may be helpful. Many of the improvements you and your peers identify can be incorporated into your job immediately (see Figure 1).

Now describe in writing each step of your diagram; this will help you articulate each step. Measure and analyze key aspects of your process. If your process has ten steps and you wish to accomplish the overall process more quickly, you might measure the amount of time required to complete each step. Record every error you encounter, keeping track of the total. These measurements allow you to establish a "baseline" from which to improve. Next, study the measurements you collect and identify ways that you can improve the process. For example, if you discovered three errors during the sixth step of your process, determine the cause of each of these errors. Perhaps the errors were caused by poor documentation of an earlier step, insufficient testing, or miscommunication with a coworker. Whatever you determine the causes to be, write them down. After you have identified the causes, list ways to eliminate them. If miscommunication with a colleague caused the error, you might eliminate this problem in the future by following up verbal communication with a written memo, or by having regular meetings to review progress.

Now you are ready to make adjustments to improve your process. Armed with information, alter your process steps to incorporate the best of your listed improvements. Next time you engage your process, you should expect the process to serve you better based on these changes. How will you know

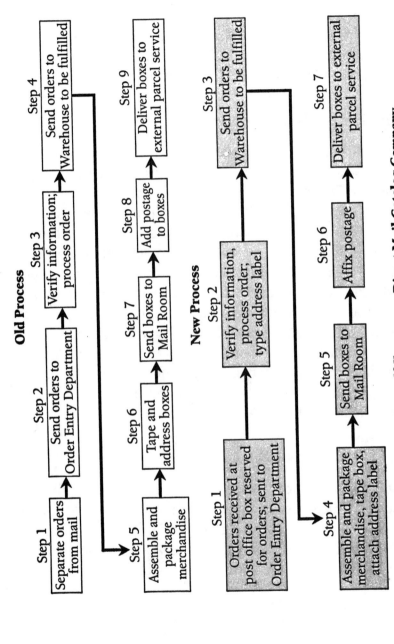

Figure 1. Order Fulfillment at a Direct Mail Catalog Company

Old Process

Step 1 — Separate orders from mail
Step 2 — Send orders to Order Entry Department
Step 3 — Verify information; process order
Step 4 — Send orders to Warehouse to be fulfilled
Step 5 — Assemble and package merchandise
Step 6 — Tape and address boxes
Step 7 — Send boxes to Mail Room
Step 8 — Add postage to boxes
Step 9 — Deliver boxes to external parcel service

New Process

Step 1 — Orders received at post office box reserved for orders; sent to Order Entry Department
Step 2 — Verify information, process order, type address label
Step 3 — Send orders to Warehouse to be fulfilled
Step 4 — Assemble and package merchandise, tape box, attach address label
Step 5 — Send boxes to Mail Room
Step 6 — Affix postage
Step 7 — Deliver boxes to external parcel service

there has been improvement? Easy, repeat the steps beginning with Step 2. Only through the discipline of continuously measuring your performance will you be certain that the process you follow is, indeed, improving.

Continuously Measure Your Progress

You may ask "Why loop back to Step 1 and not directly to Step 2 where you continue to measure key aspects of your process?" In many cases, you will probably want to loop back to Step 2. However, a process can be improved only so much. If you reach a point where the process is as finely tuned as you believe possible, yet more improvement is required to remain competitive, you need to reexamine the basic process and consider a paradigm shift. That is, consider radical new ways to perform your work. However, if you believe there is considerable improvement yet to be gained by continuing to improve the current process, then looping back to Step 2 will usually be an acceptable, even preferred, approach. These days, an organizational culture of continuous improvement is not just advantageous; it is essential.

Aim for Achievable Targets

After you have documented your process for the first time, establish measurement targets to aim for the next time you engage your process. These targets can help motivate you to achieve greater improvements. However, do not set targets that are impossible or nearly impossible to achieve.

Eliminate Defects

Continuous improvement dictates that it is no longer enough to correct a defect, you must also improve the process to prevent the defect from occurring again. A defect can be defined as a failure to meet some expected result. In the past, it was often okay to just correct the defect when it was discovered. However, today and in the future, you must also improve the process to prevent the defect from occurring again.

Do It Right the First Time

It almost always costs less to do something right the first time than to do it a second time. Many people associate "process" with bureaucracy. Although you can go overboard in documenting and implementing a process, this is not usually the problem. The problem is in establishing a process and not continuously measuring its effectiveness and adjusting as needed. An efficient process helps you enforce a concept discussed earlier—do it right the first time—in order to reduce rework and waste. Continuous improvement can help keep your company competitive—and you indispensable.

Trust Your Instincts

Everyone has great instincts—an ability to know when something is not quite right or when to take some action. Unfortunately, most people have been conditioned to rely only on objective information; consequently, they often ignore their instincts. Have you ever participated in a meeting, heard a piece of information, or operated a machine and felt strongly that something wasn't right? That the meeting participants were not understanding? That the piece of information lacked the necessary context? That the machine reacted in ways that were not user friendly—not intuitive? These are all examples of instincts at work.

Experiment With Your Instincts

Athletes provide an excellent example of how instincts can mean the difference between mediocre and excellent performance. Athletes must constantly, and instinctively, react to situations that occur too quickly for the mind to decide on a reaction. Successful athletes learn to trust their mental and physical training *and* their intuition. You might think that the instinctive reactions of an athlete are not comparable to the instincts one experiences in an office, on a manufacturing line, or with a customer. But the phenomenon is the same. Experiment and play with your instincts. You will be pleasantly surprised at the long-term benefits to your performance.

Be a Team Player, But...

The most effective teams consist of members who feel a sense of pride and ownership of the achievements of the team. When you are a member of a team, know that you are responsible for first making commitments as an individual— then as a member of a team. When you feel that a decision made by the team does not follow a legal, ethical, and fair course, don't support it. If, however, these principles are not in question but you feel the team's decision is not in the best interests of the business, work constructively to convince your team of a different solution. If you have made a sincere effort to alter the team's direction, and it was not successful, back off. As a team player you are obligated to help the team succeed. Remember that you are involved with running a business. Often a divided team is far more damaging than a misguided team.

Seek Team Success

If you act as if your success depends on your team's success, everything else will fall into place. If all your teammates also endorse this behavior, the team is all but guaranteed success. You will also find that being a fully functioning member of a well-tuned team can be a uniquely pleasurable experience and can result in friendships that can last beyond a career.

Challenge Conventional Thinking

The greatest breakthroughs and advancements in the workplace have been those that challenged the conventional thinking of the time. Impacting positive change on your team or company or industry does not have to be as profound as Galileo's demonstration that the earth rotates around the sun, or Jonas Salk's discovery of a vaccine for polio, or the Wright brothers' first airplane flight. There are unlimited opportunities of lesser magnitude that are important to your success and your company's success. Nearly everyone has some trouble challenging conventional thinking; it is easy to become stuck in a conventional thinking mode. But with practice, you can adopt the same creative thinking approaches used by visionaries in all fields. When you *do* have an unconventional idea to propose, be prepared to hear all the reasons why your idea can't possibly work (it's not in the budget, it's not your job, the boss will never go for it, etc.). Even though unconventional thinking can mean progress or breakthroughs for your company, you may face adversity in trying to change the status quo.

Everyone has a set of cognitive patterns called "paradigms" that govern their perception and, by extension, their behavior. The rules are not necessarily absolute, and in some cases are defied by objective fact, but everyone perceives their own paradigms to be "correct." Galileo experienced difficulty convincing others that the earth rotated around the sun because the common perception at that time dictated that the sun rotated around the earth. Once a "rule" becomes commonly accepted, people usually adhere to it very obstinately.

Challenge Processes, Policies, and Practices

Keep in mind that thought is the first step of any innovation. You must understand and believe that it is okay to think differently and to constantly question whether or not any given process, policy, or practice can be transformed. Once you have thought of a change you feel would be beneficial, the next step is to sell that concept to the right people. Sometimes you can put the change into motion yourself, but more often than not implementation of the change will require the assistance of other people. If you encounter resistance at this stage, don't be discouraged. Chances are that in time you will gain a reputation for creativity, ingenuity, and true dedication to the success of your company.

Be Prepared to Articulate the Pros and Cons

You must be able to articulate the benefits—short-term and long-term—of your proposal. Often in order to bring about a long-term benefit, sacrifices are necessary in the short-term. If you are honest and upfront about this, you will gain credibility as someone not just zealous about a personal interest, but concerned with the implications of change on everyone affected.

Don't Prematurely Abandon Your Proposal

Nurture your proposal until it is fully implemented and accepted. If you back off or lessen your involvement or commitment at any step along the way, your proposal may fall by the wayside. In most organizations, every responsibility can ultimately be traced to a person, an owner, a champion. And no one will champion your innovation as passionately as you.

Recover From Setbacks

A mistake is some action performed that is later judged to be in error. A setback is a temporary hindrance or reversal of progress. Everyone faces setbacks throughout each day, from misspelling a word to dropping a pencil or forgetting a name. These are typically viewed as small setbacks. What do we do? We recover and continue about our business. But people also face major setbacks from time to time. Don't be discouraged by these setbacks; you will eventually recover. If you know you will make a mistake (which you will) and you know you will eventually recover (which you will if you want to), then the major setbacks are still only temporary when put in perspective against the bigger picture of your career or life. So don't allow these setbacks to immobilize you; be ready to bounce back!

CHAPTER THREE

In Harmony:
Effective Interpersonal Communication

I believe that the best run organizations—and those with the highest morale—are typically those organizations in which people demonstrate a basic respect for one another. This chapter offers advice on how people can learn to get along with each other in the workplace regardless of the diverse backgrounds and perspectives they bring with them to the working environment. The character of an organization and of its people can be defined, in part, by the degree to which the principles described in this chapter are practiced.

Treat Others As You Would Like to Be Treated

The golden rule—simple yet powerful. The manner in which you treat other people teaches them how to treat you. If you treat people with respect from the outset of a relationship, you will most likely be treated with respect in return. The same principle applies if you treat other people with distrust, arrogance, or indifference. There is nothing magical about this principle; it is just the way human nature works.

Almost everything people know has been learned from others. People learn communication and interpersonal skills by watching family, friends, coworkers, and even television and film characters. We constantly observe, sometimes unwittingly, interpersonal communication in action. But for such an ever-present phenomenon, it's a wonder people are so underskilled in this important practice. Unfortunately, much interpersonal communication consists of two people vying to get their own way in a given situation. But mature, professional communication aims to transcend conflict and achieve a mutually beneficial end. As human beings, we are all motivated to some degree by the need for self-preservation.

But we also display strong social characteristics that allow us to achieve far greater accomplishments when we work together rather than independently. Therefore, we recognize the benefit of banding together to achieve a common goal. In fact, that's what a company is all about: providing an organized environment that allows each member to contribute unique talents to achieve a common goal. Now review the True or False quiz that begins on page 98.

Each member of a team, department, or organization should strive to strengthen the communication, not break it down. In the sections that follow, you will be introduced to tenets which, if practiced, can help create the mutual respect and harmony that is essential to maintaining high morale and a successful enterprise.

Care Enough to Listen

Listening is the greatest form of compliment. What better way to say someone is important than by giving them your undivided attention? When communicating in the workplace, the following behaviors will help you to focus your attention and show you are listening:

- Maintain frequent eye contact.
- Use body motions to show you are listening.
- Voice brief responses to show you are listening.
- Don't prematurely change the subject.
- Don't interrupt to answer your phone or to watch people pass by your doorway.
- If you do not have the time to listen to someone, let them know immediately that this is not a good time to converse.

- If you are not interested in listening to someone, tactfully let them know that you have more important priorities at the moment.

Listen

Ideas serve to broaden one's knowledge and opportunities, but you cannot consider the benefits of ideas without first listening to them. People like to cling to certain beliefs, not necessarily because they are right, but because they are comfortable. But chances are you were at one time uncomfortable with some of the ideas you embrace and espouse today. There are many more ideas that can broaden your horizons, but that you cannot consider without first listening to them. It is always your choice, and no one else's, whether or not you make these ideas part of your belief system. Listening opens up opportunities by not only strengthening business contacts and friendships but also by widening one's knowledge base both inside and outside the workplace.

Give Praise and Show Appreciation

Remember the last time someone paid you a compliment or praised you for a deed well done? How did you feel? Everyone loves to be appreciated. Recall for a moment something you achieved, something that you worked hard to attain, but for which you did not receive acknowledgment or praise—not even a passing "nice job." For many people, even the memory of the pain still rankles. Everyone hopes to be praised as a valuable member of a team or unit, but many organizations are slow to feed their employees' appetites for appreciation.

True or False?

Once again, each statement below describes a false though commonly believed notion. Review the statements and mark any that you recognize in your own day-to-day communication:

Never say "I don't know"; it is a sign of weakness.

❏ True ❏ False

Comments:

Treat a person with respect only when he or she has earned it.

❏ True ❏ False

Comments:

It is best to practice looking for the bad; that way you will be ready for anything.

❏ True ❏ False

Comments:

Never admit you're wrong.

❏ True ❏ False

Comments:

True or False? (continued)

It is acceptable to interrupt a
  conversation if what you have
  to say is more important than
  what the other person is saying.
❏ True ❏ False
Comments:

Avoid asking for help; it is a sign
  of weakness.
❏ True ❏ False
Comments:

It is better to make assumptions and
  get on with the task at hand than to
  delay by asking questions.
❏ True ❏ False
Comments:

Laughter and humor do not belong in
  a serious work environment.
❏ True ❏ False
Comments:

True or False? (continued)

Never be the first to say "hello."   ❑ True   ❑ False
Comments:

Never volunteer bad news.   ❑ True   ❑ False
Comments:

The notion of win/win is a myth;   ❑ True   ❑ False
   in every deal there is a loser.
Comments:

Praise Costs Nothing

Never underestimate the power of a kind word or deed. Its legacy lives far longer than that of material gifts. When people receive genuine praise, they are encouraged to reach further to discover the great but hidden potential within. Let's look at a few simple yet powerful measures you can take to help communicate in a positive way with those around you.

- Offer at least one compliment each day.
- Be generous in saying "thank you."
- Write an appreciative note at least once each week.
- Give praise in public (and criticism in private).
- Be quick to acknowledge the positive aspects of others' actions.
- Go out of your way to do something kind for one person each day.

Allow Others Their Golden Moments

Support your coworkers in their golden moments. Recognition, especially for the accomplishment of significant things, doesn't happen often. But when it does, a person should be encouraged to revel in and celebrate the achievement. When someone you know achieves something significant, acknowledge their accomplishment—offer a hearty handshake, a thumbs up, a note, a smile, anything that allows you to join their special celebration. Even if you hardly know the person, a well-placed comment and handshake will be remembered by that person for years to come.

Self-Giving Is Contagious

If you regularly practice these gestures, you may be amazed at their effect on the people with whom you interact. You'll delight them with your offerings and perhaps inspire them to offer appreciation as well—to you and to others. Be alert to opportunities to give praise; you will be pleased with your return on investment.

Admit When You Are Wrong

Nobody likes to be wrong, but everyone makes mistakes. Interestingly, when you are wrong, other people almost always know it. And if you do not admit your mistake, people see not only the error itself but also your reluctance to be forthcoming. When you do admit you are wrong about something, you reveal a humility that makes you more approachable. Furthermore, you can focus on making a recovery rather than mounting a defense. But something else happens when you are wrong and freely admit your mistake. The unsettling thoughts that people feel toward you and what you did immediately begin to diminish in magnitude. Real or perceived barriers come down. Consider the example below.

> The head of a small organization called a meeting to share the latest statistics on the success of the organization's products and services in the marketplace. The news was mostly gloomy, but almost everyone had seen it coming. The CEO began to publicly assess what went wrong within the organization and what could be done to solve some of

the apparent problems. But instead of opening the assessment with a salvo of accusations, he first revealed the areas in which *he* erred and discussed his plans to correct his previous mistakes. He then proceeded to identify problems from other areas of the organization and to offer suggestions for improvement.

What did the other participants of the meeting experience? Probably something that most such audiences rarely experience: someone in charge admitting to being wrong and promising to learn from his own mistakes. Like the CEO, the person who openly recognizes that mistakes happen and who works to learn from those mistakes is much more readily accepted and respected by others. Admitting to a mistake is a sign of integrity, caring, and foresight.

Be Willing to Help

Picture this: You have just been assigned a new task. You don't know everything you need to know to complete the task, but you know that several coworkers have the knowledge and skills to help you. You approach several people for assistance in those areas in which they are most adept. The scenario is probably familiar to everyone who has ever set foot in a workplace. But the outcome can be either pleasant and productive or unpleasant and fruitless, depending on the response of your coworkers.

If you don't want to meet resistance from people when you need something from them, be sure to cordially and promptly respond to their needs as well.

Four Words to Speak if You Want to Be Remembered: "I Will Help You"

The progressive organization consists of people who are quick to help one another and who understand the impact their assistance has on the overall success of the organization. Besides, it feels good to help others and it's a good habit to practice both inside and outside the workplace.

Ask for Help

Many people feel it is a sign of weakness or incompetence to ask for help or to say "I don't know." In fact, the opposite is true: It is a sign of strength and professionalism to ask for help when it is needed. There are exceptions to this rule; some people habitually depend on the assistance of others and are not otherwise able to accomplish their work. But a person who asks for some direction and then applies the information to his or her work is acting both responsibly and wisely. Let's look at an example.

Some time ago, I was in a department that was building a complex piece of computer software. About fifteen to twenty people were working on the project. A new person, Mark, joined the group about midway through the development activities. Mark seemed to spend a lot of time asking for help by asking questions about the software, the processes we were following, the tools we were using, and so on. During the first six to eight weeks, his questions were frequent and mostly basic and some people were beginning to privately question whether Mark was qualified for the job.

Throughout the next two to three months, Mark continued to ask questions, but the questions became increasingly tough. In fact, many of the questions were not easily answered by the other team members, and a few were even beyond their capacity to answer. After six months, Mark became recognized as a leading authority on the complex software being developed. Now people began to ask Mark the questions.

What happened? Mark knew that the best way to learn was to ask the people who had the answers. He may have been able to figure it out on his own, but it would have taken much longer and he would not have benefitted from others' insight. By continually asking pertinent questions and assimilating the answers, Mark became, in record time, one of the most valuable and knowledgeable members of the team.

Encourage Thoughtful Inquiry

Many people would not have been as bold and inquisitive as Mark. By asking pertinent questions whenever necessary, he exhibited both self-confidence and dedication to the team. Mark knew the value of asking for help, and in time became a valuable resource of information for others in the group.

If You Want to Learn Something, Teach It

The ability of an organization to excel is dependent on the individual skills of the team members and their ability to effectively move information from one person to another. Formidable organizations consist of strong workers who recognize and practice the need to work together and who know both when to ask for help and how to help others. When you ask someone for help, they feel needed, important, and valuable to the team. Further, when team members help each other, they develop a bond that adds to the strength of the organization as a whole. And the person being asked to help often learns something just from the experience of helping others.

Maintain a Winning Attitude

Consider this scenario: A manager has an open position in her department. The position requires a specific technical skill that is hard to find, a skill that takes years of training to proficiently learn. The manager comes across two applicants. The first applicant has an outstanding mastery of the skill but reveals a poor attitude. The second applicant has an acceptable level of mastery of the skill and has an outstanding attitude.

Which applicant is offered the job? Most astute managers will hire the qualified person who demonstrates the winning attitude, even though that person's skill level is inferior to that of the other applicant. Why? Because a team member with a bad attitude will almost always negatively influence the attitudes of coworkers. Moreover, it can be difficult, costly, and sometimes impossible to reverse a bad attitude. However, the manager of a team of people who consistently demonstrate a positive attitude knows that the team is capable of meeting extraordinary goals.

This chapter outlines positive, constructive behaviors— behaviors that can distinguish you as an indispensable employee.

A Great Attitude Makes the Difference Between Surviving and Thriving

Have you ever heard a coworker grumble, "They don't pay me enough or treat me well enough to motivate me to come in early or work late"? Where do you expect that this employee will be in five years? Whether at this company or another, the employee is likely to be no further along his or her career path and will probably still be grumbling about low pay and poor treatment by management. A good attitude in any line of business can make the difference between success and failure, in both personal and professional endeavors. A winning attitude helps to improve productivity, enhance communication, reduce stress, and open the door to new opportunity.

Take Charge of Your Attitude

You are free to choose the way you think. If you doubt the power of a great attitude, try expressing one for a full day. If you are not used to doing this, it might be a struggle, but you are sure to be wonderfully surprised at how you are treated by coworkers, customers, friends, and family. Now work at improving your attitude for a week.

WARNING!
A good attitude can be habit-forming.

Eliminate Anger

Anger is a powerful, destructive emotion that weakens and sometimes destroys relationships both in the workplace and outside it. People list any number of rationalizations for their anger, but it is rarely justified. There are alternative behaviors that are far more productive and much less stressful for everyone involved. Work to eliminate anger from your life. This does not mean that instead you will allow people to exploit you—far from it. Anger signifies a loss of control, and when this occurs, a person is most vulnerable. When people choose an alternate response, they are able to remain in control of their emotions and of the situation at hand. As difficult as it may be in the heat of the moment, focus on solving the *problem* that has arisen, *not* on the person or persons involved.

Maintain a Generous Supply of Humor

It is well recognized that humor contributes to the health and well-being of a person. But humor is also good for the health and well-being of an organization. People work more effectively and efficiently when they are having fun. Tasteful humor is a welcomed and permissible form of communication within the organization.

Humor can strengthen bonds between people and greatly ease the tension that is so prevalent in today's workplace. Learn to laugh throughout the day. *Find* something to laugh about and allow yourself to laugh about it. Humor helps dispel stress, fear, intimidation, and a host of other workplace maladies. But remember to use your wit to amuse, not abuse, other people. Avoid the use of sarcasm or otherwise biting humor.

Bottom line? Loosen up! Problems are only as big or as serious as a person perceives them to be, and when put in perspective of the bigger picture can almost always be made appreciably lighter.

Recognize and Celebrate Diversity

The modern workplace comprises people of diverse backgrounds who come together in support of a common cause. It is virtually impossible for one person to know all, see all, or be all. In fact, the strength of a team lies not in the number of members but in their diversity of skills and talents.

Recall some of the problems that your team has faced in the past. Chances are that in each instance your team relied on a diverse range of skills—provided by various members— to address and solve the problem. The greater the diversity of the team, the more versatile will be its contributions to the organization.

Basic Etiquette Tips When Greeting People

A common myth is that the higher a person's position in the company, the more respect he or she should receive. I don't agree. Everyone, regardless of their position, deserves to be treated with respect. The first opportunity you have to acknowledge the importance of another person is when you are greeting them, whether for the first time ever or the fifth time that day. These simple gestures not only help you to look and feel good, but will have the same effect on the person you greet.

1. Remember and use people's first names.

2. When meeting someone for the first time, extend your hand and give your name. If you are seated, stand to greet them. Remember their name and use it occasionally during the conversation.
3. Frequently look people in the eye.
4. Be quick to smile.
5. Be the first to say hello.

Consider the Impact of Your Words

As tools of communication, words can serve both constructive and destructive ends. Words are used to offer praise, education, constructive criticism, and concern. They are also used to relay gossip, lies, destructive criticism, and anger. The words people choose and the manner in which they deliver them tell as much about the communicator as about the information relayed.

Take Responsibility for Your Manner of Communication

Two of the toughest lessons of the workplace are learning when to speak and when not to speak and what to say and what not to say. Everyone can no doubt recall some incident in which they communicated in a manner that they later regretted. Unfortunately, words cannot be retrieved.

Below are some guidelines for appropriate, productive use of speech:

■ Avoid gossip, fresh or used.
■ Do not speak ill of others.

- Use tact in all remarks; show consideration for people's feelings.
- Learn when to remain silent.
- Learn when to speak.
- Relay your message in the fewest words possible.
- Do not distort facts.
- Give credit where due.
- Keep your voice at a comfortable level.
- Do not interrupt other people while they are talking.

Make Your Leader a Hero

This topic is consistently one of the least expected among the audiences I address on the topics presented in this book. People are surprised that I would advise them to focus their attention not on themselves or their team, but on their manager. After all, don't managers get enough attention and credit as it is? It might help to understand how I stumbled upon this notion.

Years ago, I was a systems programmer in a department that was developing a new computer operating system. The department ran into difficulties with the schedules and costs and a seasoned development manager was selected to take over. My first encounter with my new manager was brief but to the point. He said he was assigning me to a staff position and that my principal task was to make him a hero.

My first impression was "Where did they get this arrogant, self-centered person?" But I decided to do my best to help make the manager look good. For the next several weeks I was actively involved in resolving problems both within and outside the department. All my actions stemmed from the objective that all problems should be resolved in favor of my manager's interests.

Something began to happen that I hadn't expected: Work began to run more smoothly, and my boss began to look good in the eyes of others. By focusing on the interests of my manager, I found it much easier to resolve problems. I came to realize that if my manager was successful, then so too would be the product we developed, the team, the team members, and of course, the company.

I have continued to apply this perspective over the years in my own work and have consistently seen positive results. My experience indicates that people are more driven to meet commitments to *people* than to events, dates, or tasks. Occasionally an audience member at a presentation will say "But you don't know my boss! If I make him look good, he will take all the credit and run!" My reply is that there are some rotten apples out there, but they are the exception rather than the rule. The majority of managers will do the honorable thing and acknowledge the team and those people who contributed the most to the overall success of the enterprise.

Attack Problems, Not People

When your team or organization is faced with a problem, the best thing you can do is work to solve it. The worst thing you can do is to attack the person who discovers or owns the problem. After the problem is solved or well on its way to being solved, the person who owned the problem should be asked how the problem, or a similar problem, might best be prevented in the future. Changes to the process should be made to help avert a recurrence of the problem. The person who learned from his or her mistake should be praised and encouraged to move ahead.

This process fits the model of continuous improvement and will likely result in the following:

- The team members will focus their energy on solving the problem.
- The process that allowed the problem is improved so that the problem is less likely to recur.
- The owner of the problem has learned from the experience.
- The owner of the problem maintains dignity and respect because of the way he or she was treated by the other employees.
- People will not hesitate to address problems in the future.

Eliminate Surprises

With the exception of an occasional birthday or congratulations party, don't surprise your boss, your peers, or your subordinates. Even good news sprung on someone unexpectedly can be dangerous.

One manager received notification from the personnel department that a promotion and accompanying salary increase for one of his employees had just been approved. He was now free to tell his employee about the promotion. An organizational meeting was planned for that afternoon and the manager decided to surprise the employee with the good news in front of fifty peers. Unfortunately, the employee was going through a nasty divorce and did not want his spouse to learn of the promotion and salary increase. At the announcement of the news, the employee was disturbed rather than delighted.

Of course, surprising people with good news does not always elicit an unpleasant reaction, but keep in mind that it *can* backfire. Most surprises in the workplace have to do with bad news and thus it is essential that the messenger be sensitive to the timing and manner of delivery.

Disclose Bad News in a Private Setting

If you surprise someone—whether your peer, your boss, or your subordinate—in a public forum, the person may be embarrassed, angry, or otherwise put off guard. And you, as the messenger, will not win any praise for tact. Before delivering unpleasant news, ask yourself, "If I had to receive this bad news, how would I prefer to learn about it?" Depending on the severity of the news, most people would rather be briefed in a private or semi-private setting. Further, allow the receiver of the news the opportunity to privately disclose the information to the other people who need to know.

Disclose Bad News As Soon As Possible

Bad news is like spoiled food—the longer the delay in taking action, the bigger the stink. Usually the best policy is to disclose the news early. The longer you delay, the greater the likelihood that the reaction will be amplified. Of course, when revealing bad news, it's also important to be able to show a recovery plan (if applicable) or say you are working on one to be available by a given date.

❙ ❙ ❚ Exercise 10 ❚ ❙ ❙
Skillful Communication

Recall three or four instances in which you said something you later wished you hadn't. Briefly describe each incident in the space provided below. Now examine the use of speech guidelines on pages 110-111 and note any that apply to the regrettable situations. How could observation of one or more of the guidelines have prevented you from saying something you later regretted?

Incident	Relevant Guidelines	Rank

Next, go through the ten guidelines and rank them in order of their relevance to your own personal and professional growth. In other words, the comment marked "1" should be the guideline you believe you most need to improve in practice. Make an effort to honor the guidelines at work, home, and wherever else you go. Especially keep in mind the suggestions you ranked highly.

This simple exercise can considerably raise your awareness of the impact your words have on other people. Even a careful study of these guidelines is, of course, no guarantee that you won't again say something you later regret, but a review of the list from time to time will help you remain aware of verbal minefields.

❚ ❚ ❚

The best work environments are those in which the team members can openly and honestly share unpleasant news as it occurs. You may not have control over the news itself, but you can act responsibly with regard to the timing and manner of disclosure.

Ask Questions Rather Than Assume

Have you ever assumed something and later learned you were wrong? We all have. Many incorrect assumptions that you make on the job probably cost your company considerable rework, lost time, and, ultimately, lost revenue. Let's look at some examples of common assumptions.

- An employee assumes she will receive a good evaluation because her manager doesn't ever give feedback about how to improve. Instead, the employee receives a low evaluation.
- A manufacturing employee assumes that a specially ordered device is specified in meters rather than feet and manufactures an incorrectly sized device.
- A computer programmer assumes he knows the programming interface to another person's program because it seems so logical, but loses many days of development and testing because the interface did not work.
- An administrative employee assumes that another member of a meeting will reserve the conference room, but instead the meeting must be delayed until the meeting room is next available.

Becoming an Indispensable Employee

■ A project director assumes that a supplier will deliver a set of much-needed components because the supplier agreed to the delivery date of two months. However, he does not receive the components because the supplier, having had no communication from the project director in the interim, assumes the shipment can be delivered late.

An Ounce of Prevention Is Worth a Pound of Cure

It is important to spend five minutes asking questions rather than lose five days on a schedule or five thousand dollars in business opportunity. I have personally *never* met anyone who enjoys doing the same thing twice: wrong the first time and right the second. But how can a person tell if it is best to ask the question? Let's look at some general guidelines.

Ask a question when you have the opportunity to

■ Prevent repetition of a job, or significant rework

■ Avoid missing a commitment

■ Keep yourself or someone else from looking bad

■ Save money

■ Save time

■ Learn and improve

■ Avoid confusion and misunderstanding

■ Make the difference between success and failure

If one or more of the situations above applies, ask the question. If you aren't sure, ask the question.

Remove the Need for Others to Assume

So far, we have focused on the need for you to ask questions rather than risk making incorrect assumptions. But you can help other people not to make assumptions about the work and interactions you share with them. When you request a service, give a directive, or provide advice, give others clear and complete information. Do not assume that something obvious to you is obvious to someone else. After your dialogue with the person, ask him or her to replay what he thought he heard you say. Exercise tact as you do this. Let the other person know that your objective is flawless communication. This small demonstration not only helps ensure the job will be done right the first time, but also strengthens the support others give you. Both of you will feel good about one another's contributions in communicating and getting the job done.

Adopt a Set of "People Principles"

This chapter has focused mainly on your personal behavior in the workplace. Although one person *can* influence change in an organization, the more employees that rally behind a cause, the stronger will be its impact. To this end, develop a set of People Principles to be adopted across your organization (or your team if you choose to start on a smaller scale).

The principles might start with the tenets described in this chapter. Then add your own ideas that focus on important areas within your organization. One approach for starting this list might be to assemble a small team. The members should represent various teams or departments from across the organization and have the support of management. You may want to discuss this plan initially with your own manager and then with the manager of Human Resource Development. The objective of the team is to develop a list of People Principles and then to propose to management that all employees participate in a training program based on the principles. Once the proposal is accepted, every member of the organization should be trained to understand and apply the People Principles. In fact, management might choose to make adherence to the People Principles an evaluation criterion in appraising the performance of employees.

Because an organization consists of people of diverse background and experience, these principles may not be intuitively obvious to everyone. If they were, organizations would not have so many people-related problems. If you anticipate resistance from management to adopt these principles across the organization, you might want to revisit the first chapter for encouragement on taking a risk, not fearing failure, and dealing with criticism. You can make it happen...if you choose to!

CHAPTER FOUR

Treat Everyone As a Customer:
Internal and External Service

A lot has been written in recent years about the importance of customer service in keeping an organization afloat. It goes without saying that any conscientious employee will espouse the guidelines discussed in the last section of this chapter for giving superior service to the customers of an organization. But this chapter focuses not so much on these external customers as on those people within your organization whom you serve in the course of your daily work. The chapter forwards the notion of service to an *internal* customer—the person or department that receives a product or service from you. *Everyone* who is employed has one or more internal customers.

Most employees do not commonly regard the people in their organizations as "customers" and as a result do not always offer the same level of service that they would to someone paying for a product or service. But if you can learn to view the people whose needs you serve in the organization as customers, you can greatly enhance the interaction you have with them. To encourage a customer service mindset, this chapter uses the term "customer" in place of manager, colleague, or team.

Examine Yourself As a Customer

You are a customer every day of your life. You consume products and services not only when you are watching television, grocery shopping, riding public transit, etc., but also when you use the products and services within your company or organization. You are a customer to fellow employees who may be within earshot, down the hall, or across the country. Take a few moments to reflect on what customer service—internal or external—means to you. What

True or False?

The following statements all relate to working with internal customers. As before, the statements reflect common notions, none of which are true. As you read the statements, ask yourself how often you subscribe to these misconceptions in your own relations with customers.

A customer is someone who pays for a
product or service. ☐ True ☐ False

Comments:

Internal customers do not expect
the same treatment as external
customers. ☐ True ☐ False

Comments:

Internal customer satisfaction has
nothing to do with job security. ☐ True ☐ False

Comments:

True or False? (continued)

It is important to have a good attitude
toward external customers, but with
internal customers you can "be yourself."   □ True   □ False

Comments:

It is the customer's responsibility to
give feedback about service.   □ True   □ False
Comments:

You know your customers' wants and
needs better than they do.   □ True   □ False
Comments:

Never offer help to a customer unless it
is solicited.   □ True   □ False
Comments:

are some examples of good service you have experienced? Bad service? Have you ever discontinued use of a product or service because of poor treatment? Have you ever confronted someone who has given you poor service?

Understand Your Customers' Wants and Needs

What are "wants" and "needs"? These terms are often used loosely and deserve some elaboration. "Needs" are conditions that a customer believes must be met in order for him or her to be minimally satisfied. "Wants" are things that your customer can live without, but would prefer to have. How can you learn what your customers' wants and needs really are? Ask them! If you ask and then listen, you will probably learn far more than you imagined. Here are the basic steps to follow in learning what your customers really want and need.

1. Solicit and write down the products or services your customers expect.
2. Compare the information you gather with what you now provide.
3. Propose improvements in weak areas.
4. Verify that the proposed solutions will satisfy your customers' expectations. If not, make the appropriate changes.
5. Implement the solutions.
6. Measure the effectiveness of the solutions and continuously survey your customers for their satisfaction with your products and services.
7. Go back to Step 2.

Define Your Customer

In the space below, list all the people within your organization to whom you provide a product or service. In the second column, describe what you offer to them, and in the third mark how often you provide the product or service.

Customer	Product/Service	How Often?
1.		
2.		
3.		
4.		
5.		
6.		
7.		
8.		
9.		
10.		

█ █ █

▎ ▌ ▐ Exercise 12 ▐ ▌ ▎
Whose Customer Are You?

In the space provided, list all the people, departments, and organizations of which you are a customer. In the second column, list what products or service they provide, and in the third column, evaluate the service you receive from them on a scale of one to ten. You can make notes next to the rating to support your evaluation.

Supplier	Product/Service	Rating	Comments
1.			
2.			
3.			
4.			
5.			
6.			
7.			
8.			
9.			
10.			

▌ ▌ ▌

Let's examine each of these steps.

1. **Solicit and write down the products or services your customers expect.**

   For example, say you work for a company that builds "figments." The process of building a figment consists of ten steps, each performed by a different department. Your department is responsible for the fourth step and your customer is the department responsible for the fifth step. You ask your customers what they expect from you when you deliver your product to them. The answers to your questions point to four key areas of expectations: a certified inspection, a defect-free product, any unique handling instructions that would be helpful, and delivery within the defined time and cost constraints.

2. **Compare the information you gather with what you now provide.**

   Focus on those areas in which you believe you are not currently satisfying your customers' expectations. Looking back to the example, you find that your product is not always formally inspected. The product is often delivered with known defects that impact your customer's processing time. Special instructions are not always passed along. You typically deliver your product about 25 percent later than planned. Your costs are usually about 20 percent higher than expected.

3. **Propose improvements in weak areas.**

   Be prepared to consider some radical changes, even those that might be costly. However, make sure your proposals are based on a sound understanding of your ability to deliver. Back to the example: You propose a mandatory twenty-point inspection checklist to be conducted and certified with the inspector's signature. Inspection of the twenty items is expected to catch the most common defects that have been slipping by. Only after the correction of all defects found will the inspection be certified complete. The inspection includes reviewing—for completion and accuracy—any instructions that must be passed along to the next step of the process. The last step of the inspection measures the time and cost of the fourth step. If either is more than planned, a formal review of the department's process is conducted and suggested improvements are made to reduce the cost and time allotment for the next product.

4. **Verify that the proposed solutions will satisfy your customers' expectations.**

    Unless you are very sure of your proposals, you should show them to your customers to make sure the proposals will satisfy the customers' needs and most important wants. Work with your customers to alter the proposals until you are comfortable that you will achieve the desired level of customer satisfaction. Looking again at the example, you receive feedback from your customers that indicates your proposals will satisfy all major areas of concern except one: the inspection process. To resolve the problem, you agree to allow your customers to participate as members of the inspection team and also as members of the group that reviews the department's processes whenever examination is warranted.

5. Implement the solutions.

Implement the proposed solutions—all of them. Once you have involved your customers, they will expect you to follow up and implement the agreed-upon recommendations. Take this action swiftly and visibly. Let your customers know that you care about them and appreciate their cooperation and participation. Let them know that you will continue to invest in their satisfaction.

6. Measure the effectiveness of the solutions and continuously survey your customers for their satisfaction with your products and services.

Establish a routine method of soliciting feedback from your customers to ensure that your efforts address your customers' greatest wants and needs. A word of caution: Don't always assume that your customer is the expert or knows best. Carefully measure your performance to ensure you are making the anticipated progress. Don't be surprised if you learn that some recommended ideas did far less to improve customer satisfaction than expected. It is important to continuously measure success and to correct those actions that are not yielding the expected return on investment.

7. Go back to Step 2.

Now go back to Step 2 and repeat the last six steps. If you feel your customers' wants and needs have changed—as they often will—then return to Step 1 instead. Make the continuous exercise of these seven steps an integral part of your internal customer satisfaction process.

A Note About External Customers

The procedure above can be used with external customers of your organization as well, if you are in a position of serving them either directly or indirectly. In today's hypercompetitive business environment, no organization can afford to give poor service to its customers. While countless resources address the topic of customer service—books, videotapes, training programs—the following guidelines highlight some universal principles. Follow the ten guidelines in your daily interactions with external customers, whether in person, on the phone, or through correspondence. Many of the tips lend themselves to internal customer service as well. The list is by no means exhaustive but offers several of the most basic and essential principles of customer contact.

Ten Rules of Customer Contact

1. **Display a great attitude and, if meeting face to face, smile and use direct eye contact.**

   People enjoy being around a person with a positive, enthusiastic attitude. It's contagious. If you are communicating in person, be generous with your smile and don't hesitate to establish eye contact. This helps to give the customer a feeling of importance. You want your customers to have a good experience every time they do business with you. Every time!

2. **Ensure your appearance is clean, acceptable, and appropriate to your position.**

   Your hygiene and dress should not be offensive or distracting to your customer. Keep your attire clean, suitably modest, and in good condition. There are, of course, exceptions to this rule, such as in the case of employees who work outdoors or with machinery.

Being overdressed can also be unacceptable. Depending on the industry, many customers are more comfortable when confronted by people who are not overdressed.

3. **Offer help before it is requested.**

If you work in the type of business where people can browse, give them the space to do so after you have asked them if they would like assistance. Some people want to be left alone but most will appreciate your willingness to help. Many people *are* looking for some assistance, even if only a pointer to another aisle, item, or idea.

4. **When with a customer, give your full attention.**

Once you have engaged a customer, give that customer your full attention. Don't flit between customers or tasks unless the customer wants time alone. While you might be busy and doing the best you can, your customer has one purpose in coming to you and, therefore, is very sensitive to not receiving the same focused attention in return. If you find yourself in a situation where your customer must wait for you, continually let your customer know that you have not forgotten him or her. The objective is to keep the channel of communication open and to send a strong signal that says "your business is important to me."

5. **Immediately seek help if you cannot satisfy your customer's question or problem.**

If you cannot answer a customer's query, don't stop there. Go for help. Show your customers that you are willing to go out of your way to accommodate them. Seek out the answer to their question or problem as expeditiously as you can. You will not only please your customer, but will also learn something for the next time the problem or question arises.

6. **Make available a channel for your customer to communicate with your superior.**

   Make it easy for a customer to go over your head to complain about poor service or praise you for great service. If a customer asks to see your superior, immediately find your boss. If your boss is not available, confirm that you will ask your boss to get in touch with the customer as soon as possible.

7. **Meet or beat your commitments.**

   If you tell your customer you will call back in ten minutes—do it. If you say the document or the car or the loan will be available at 3 p.m.—make it so. If your product or service is ready earlier than expected, let your customer know so that he or she has the option of responding earlier.

8. **Never deliver a defective product or service without the customer's knowledge.**

   Never ship mistakes out the door without warning your customers of the problem. Some defects might not bother customers, but the decision should always be theirs to make. Your customers will sense and appreciate your passion for quality—a reputation that will serve you well.

9. **Say "thank you" and acknowledge that you appreciate the customer's business.**

   After a sale or transaction, always say "thank you" while looking the customer in the eye. If there is no sale, let your prospective customers know that you appreciate their consideration of your products and services and that you will be happy to serve them in the future.

10. **If appropriate, follow up with your customer to measure his or her satisfaction and offer assistance if needed.**

    It is far easier to keep a customer than to find a new one. After customers have used a product or service of yours, it is helpful to solicit feedback to measure their satisfaction. If you come across a customer who is not pleased, immediately work to correct the problem. Unless you follow up with your customers, you will never know whether or not they are truly satisfied.

You might find it helpful to discuss these ten rules among your peers. Take liberties to alter the list to suit your work environment. This helps to raise the level of sensitivity and awareness of all those who work alongside you. If your colleagues look good to your customers, so will you and your organization. You don't represent only yourself or your department; to the external customer, you *are* the company!

CHAPTER FIVE

Your Menu of Skills: Making the Right Choice

W ill your job—the one you have now, or even the one you have your eye on—be there for as long as you want it? For virtually everyone, the answer is a resounding "NO!" Not only will the same job not be there, but for many people, their need for a job will outlast the company that currently employs them.

Don't Expect Your Job—or Even Your Company—to Always Be There for You

Most employees now realize that the unwritten contract that once existed between employee and employer is largely void in today's work environment. Neither the employer nor the employee can guarantee that work will be permanent. Consequently, the ability to continuously enhance your skill value will make you more valuable as an employee and more marketable should you find yourself looking for work.

> Skill value is defined here as a person's worth to an employer based on his or her ability to satisfy the particular needs of the employer.

Read the definition carefully. It does not mean that if you have strong skills in various areas everyone will want to employ you. It means you must have the skills *sought* by the employer.

The Right Skills Are More Valuable Than a Multitude of Skills

If you want to climb the ladder of success, be prepared to furnish your own ladder. That is, take responsibility for developing those skills necessary to attain your goals. This chapter helps you to better understand your skill value in your current job or in a job that you hope to eventually attain. This chapter also helps you to understand how to continuously improve your skill value so that you find yourself in a favorable position when opportunity knocks—or when you create opportunity. Your skill value has a direct impact on your ability to both stay employed and obtain new employment.

For your company to be competitive, it must have employees who have competitive skills. The indispensable employee takes a proactive role in acquiring and using the appropriate skills. If you wait for your manager or company to initiate skill enhancement, you may find that the encouragement is written on a pink slip. Read on to learn more about what you can do to help yourself and your organization become more competitive.

Develop a Competitive Edge: A Menu of Skills

The best way to become and remain competitive in your company is to acquire and demonstrate the skills that your company needs to be successful. These words are disarmingly simple, yet they bear repeating. It is necessary to be proactive, to determine what skills are necessary, and then to pursue them, even if that means incurring some of the expense and training on your own time. If your newfound capacities are in fact related to your work, you will inevitably have the opportunity to use them on the job. During times of struggle, most companies trim their work force. Even during prosperous times, organizations frequently undergo strategic changes aimed at strengthening the company's competitive posture. Who gets trimmed first? From what I've seen, it's usually the people who demonstrate the weakest skills, or have the most replaceable skills—regardless of how long they have been employed. Further, the employees of poorly performing departments also tend to be targeted for dismissal. This fact offers yet another reason to pursue not only individual success but also the overall success of your team or department.

Obtain a Competitive Skill Level

A company must have the best trained, best skilled employees to become and remain competitive. And the criteria continue to grow. If a company's best resource is its people, it is the skills of those people that allow a company to improve quality, improve productivity, reduce costs, reduce production and delivery time, improve customer satisfaction, increase market share, and increase profit. Further, if your skill level is not competitive within your organization, it probably is not competitive outside of it.

Continuously Improve Your Skill Value

This may mean being totally retrained and learning entirely new skills. You must have competitive skills. This has nothing to do with outdoing your peers or becoming cutthroat in your work relationships. It simply means you must have the skills that your employer needs. Loyalty is an important part of serving a company. Every company wants it and, in many cases, demands it. However, loyalty is not the major criterion for getting or keeping a job. It certainly helps, but your ongoing skill value is the overriding factor.

True or False?

As you review the following statements (all of which are false but commonly believed) consider whether you endorse them in your own views and behavior.

Once a person has been trained in a
   particular field, it is unwise to
   consider changing fields.
Comments:
       ❏ True   ❏ False

Organizations, not individuals, are
   responsible for developing careers.
Comments:
       ❏ True   ❏ False

Loyalty assures job security.
Comments:
       ❏ True   ❏ False

Competitive skills are not as important
   as willingness to do a good job.
Comments:
       ❏ True   ❏ False

Skill enhancement is an added value;
    it is not requisite to superior job
    performance.   ❏ True   ❏ False
Comments:

Full-time employment precludes the
    time necessary for skill enhancement   ❏ True   ❏ False
    training.
Comments:

The best time to seek skill enhance-
    ment training is when one is not   ❏ True   ❏ False
    employed.
Comments:

Employees who volunteer for extra
    training do not have enough work   ❏ True   ❏ False
    to do.
Comments:

Employees should not be expected to
    forgo personal time or money for   ❏ True   ❏ False
    skill enhancement.
Comments:

Try to develop a menu of skills. The more versatile you become in the skills needed by your employer, the more indispensable you become. In this age of empowerment, being a specialist in one or two capacities is hardly noteworthy. Decide the technical and interpersonal skills that will serve you best in your field and work to develop them. In addition, look for better ways to do your job and to simplify core operations.

Don't become complacent about your current skills. Many of the skills in high demand today will be obsolete in a few years. Even "experts" must continually undergo skill enrichment to keep up with the rapid changes affecting virtually every industry.

Individuals chart their own careers; companies and mentors assist. As the saying goes, "Luck is what happens when preparation meets opportunity." The menu of skills that you offer is the primary factor that figures in your value as an employee.

Don't Put Off Improving and Expanding Your Skills

"Okay," you say. "If continual improvement and skill enhancement is so important, why do I find it so difficult to set aside time and energy to focus on this area? Why do I keep putting it off?" Let's look at some of the more common reasons for this behavior:

You still have your job. As long as the paychecks keep coming, it is easy to believe there is no reason to step outside the ordinary routine. But as anyone who has lost a job for any reason can tell you, the change can occur suddenly, with little if any prior warning.

You can't find time during normal work hours, and you don't want to give up any personal time. The quality of life you desire must be earned, and some amount of sacrifice is usually required. Talk to your manager about creating a window of time for training, and if it is not possible, complete the training on your own time.

You feel you're too old to change. Whether you've been on the job for five years or fifty years, you feel you've been away from formal training so long that you are now incapable of learning "new tricks." But the truth is that the brain is perfectly capable of continuous learning; give it a chance.

You don't feel you deserve the attention and investment. You may have resigned yourself to being a low-potential employee; after all, this resignation reduces risk and stress. But are you genuinely satisfied with this decision? Isn't the fact that you are reading this book evidence to the contrary?

You are afraid of more responsibility. Skill enhancement often results in more responsibility and accountability on the job. Welcome this opportunity; it will enhance both your personal and your professional growth.

You feel you cannot afford the loss of money that retraining will cause. In today's lean times, this concern is legitimate. But skill enhancement is an *investment* in your future; budget for it as you would any other low-risk, high-return venture.

You are satisfied with your current salary and position. If this applies to you, congratulations. You have found fulfilling work. Nevertheless, there is every possibility that skill enhancement will be necessary to *keep* this job in the future.

You don't know which skills need to be enhanced. If no one has told you what skills are or will become pertinent to your job, ask your manager. Although you may be justified in believing that it is your organization's responsibility to inform you if further training is necessary, you are better off being proactive.

The people who will have the most secure jobs tomorrow are improving their skill value today. Each of the reasons listed above may have some validity, but it is the aim of this book to teach you not to rely on the status quo. You cannot afford to wait for opportunity to knock; you need to open the door yourself. The people who will have the most secure jobs tomorrow are improving their skill value today.

Define Your Skill Needs

This section offers an approach you can use to identify the skills you need for your current job, your next job, or your ultimate job. First, you must decide your priorities at this point in your career. If your priority is to become more secure in your current job, then you need to focus your attention on strengthening the skills for that job. If you are interested in planning for your "dream" job, you need to focus on acquiring the skills pertinent to *that* position.

Some companies have processes in place to help their employees identify the skills they need to enhance or acquire. If you work for such a company, follow the standard procedure and use the steps below as a checklist. If you don't work for a company with an established process for skill enhancement, follow the steps below.

1. Identify the skills required. List the skills necessary to satisfactorily perform the job you have chosen. In many cases, your manager can be a big help in this step; ask your manager what skills he or she examines in evaluating job performance. If you are aiming for a new position, it is even more important to get help in identifying the skills relevant to this job. If possible, ask your manager to put you in touch with whoever is the most valuable resource of information for the job: perhaps another manager or the personnel department.

As you list the skills, try to cover all aspects of the job. Let's look at an example: A sales clerk at a retail department store is interested in becoming a department manager. With the help of his manager, he concludes that knowledge of the following areas is required for the next job:

- Merchandise
- Customer psychology
- Profit and loss, and cost accounting
- Planning and organizing
- Order entry and inventory control
- Local, state, and federal consumer laws
- Personnel practices of hiring, training, evaluating, rewarding, and firing

2. Identify the level of proficiency that is needed for each skill. This step requires a rating system to indicate proficiency levels. Let's use the rating scale on the following page.

1 = requires very little or no knowledge

2 = requires some knowledge

3 = requires considerable knowledge

4 = requires expert knowledge

As in Step 1, you may wish to ask for assistance from someone who understands the job you are aiming for. Let's continue with our example: The sales clerk, with some help from his manager, identifies the level of proficiency required for the skills identified in Step 1. The rating value follows the skill.

Knowledge of the merchandise: 3

Knowledge of customer psychology: 3

Knowledge of profit and loss, and cost accounting: 3

Knowledge of planning and organization: 3

Knowledge of order entry and inventory control: 4

Knowledge of local, state, and federal consumer laws: 2

Knowledge of personnel practices of hiring, training, evaluating, rewarding, and firing: 3

---

3. Identify your current proficiency in the relevant skills. This step does not require that you randomly list every skill you have. Rather, the purpose is to examine the skills listed in Step 2 and identify your proficiency level. The rating scale is similar to that used for Step 2:

1 = little or no knowledge

2 = some knowledge

3 = considerable knowledge

4 = expert knowledge

Although you can accomplish this step individually, you may want to supplement your own assessment with that of a manager or peer. In other words, once you've evaluated your proficiency in each area, ask someone you work with to give his or her perception of how well your current skills match your perception. If this assessment varies greatly from your own, address this difference before going on to the next step. Returning to our example, the results might look like the following. The first number relates to the required rating, the second to the sales clerk's self-perception.

Knowledge of the merchandise: 3, 3

Knowledge of customer psychology: 3, 2

Knowledge of profit and loss, and cost accounting: 3, 1

Knowledge of planning and organization: 3, 2

Knowledge of order entry and inventory control: 4, 3

Knowledge of local, state, and federal consumer laws: 2, 1

Knowledge of personnel practices of hiring, training, evaluating, rewarding, and firing: 3, 1

---

4. Identify those skills that need enhancement. Now identify those skills that need enhancement by comparing the two proficiency ratings for each skill listed in the previous steps. A rating lower than the rating required indicates a need for improvement in the given skill area. Continuing with the example, the sales clerk already meets the requirements for the first skill area listed (knowledge of the merchandise), but needs improvement in the remaining six areas before he will be considered competitive for the position of department manager.

Now that these four steps are complete, where do you go from here? You have listed the skills that you need to enhance or acquire. It is very likely that your list will be longer than the list shown in the abbreviated example. However, don't be discouraged by the length of the list. It is far better to understand what you need and where you are going than to blindly stumble forward on mostly assumptions, hope, and expectations. Also recognize that the example and rating system focuses on knowledge, not experience. Many jobs require working knowledge—experience—for some skills. For example, if you are interested in competing for a job as a commercial airline pilot, you need not only knowledge of how to fly a plane but also thousands of hours of actual flying experience. To keep the above example simple, the dimension of experience was purposely omitted; however, in completing the skill evaluation for yourself, try to include a similar rating for work experience.

Before leaving this section, ask yourself the following three personal questions:

1. What do I like to do or think I would like to do?
2. What am I good at or think I would be good at?
3. What don't I like to do or think I would not like to do?

It has been my experience that people usually perform well at those undertakings they enjoy. This combination of proficiency and enjoyability usually makes for a great personal attitude. All this in turn directly influences productivity, quality, and overall contribution. Therefore, in deciding what skills you need to enhance, factor in your level of interest for each of the undertakings.

Enrich Your Skills

The previous section explained how to identify the skills needed for a particular career path. This section presents ideas to help you pursue your identified objectives—those activities that can enhance your skill value in the areas in which you have the greatest interest. All of these ideas will help you improve your skill value, while some will help you influence others in improving their skill value as well.

Seek On-the-Job Training Opportunities

Seek out tasks within your company that will both utilize some of the skills you have already developed and require you to learn new ones. I believe that the majority of people learn most of what they know from on-the-job training. You can substantially accelerate this learning by taking on assignments of varied skill requirements.

Participate in Your Company's Educational Offerings

Many larger companies have an education or training department to develop or lead classes for employees. This department is likely to welcome special requests for classes and seminars. Let the department head know the specific skill training or continuous education you are seeking. Don't overlook on-line computer tutorials; these computer-assisted tutorials are available to teach basic word processing skills as well as more specialized training such as computer graphics, marketing tactics, and basic accounting.

Take Classes

If the classes you are looking for are not available through your company, check community colleges and universities. Many classes are offered during both the day and early evening. Some companies have programs that will reimburse an employee for all or part of the schooling. If your company does not have a standard policy, speak to your manager about reimbursement for the skills training you are undergoing on your own time. Be prepared to describe the value to the company of this outside education.

Read Trade Journals, Industry Newsletters, and Books

Read the latest information in your areas of interest. If you have a company library, take advantage of its offerings, as well as those of the local public library. This measure will keep you up to date on trends and movements in your field and give you ideas to apply to your own job.

Attend Trade Shows, Conferences, and Seminars

Find out the latest in what suppliers, vendors, competitors, and industry specialists have to offer. These events typically run from one to three days. Afterward, write a report on the event so your peers can also benefit from your experience.

Offer to present a summary to your department, team, or company.

Join Professional Societies

Professional societies exist for virtually every professional field and area of interest. Membership to these societies provides the opportunity to exchange ideas with people in your field and is a valuable networking tool. If a chapter does not exist in your community, consider working with other interested people to start one.

Subscribe to an Electronic Bulletin Board

Also known as computer forums, these on-line bulletin boards provide a handy and usually responsive method to exchange problems, solutions, and ideas among like-minded people from other companies and even countries. If the benefits of this forum are apparent to your manager, and you would like to spend most of your forum time outside of normal working hours, perhaps your manager would support your use of a company-owned computer at home.

Invite Special Speakers

Through the appropriate department within your company, invite speakers and instructors to present seminars and classes. If possible, see that the educational opportunities are available to coworkers during regular working hours. It is far less expensive for your company to bring a speaker or class to the employees than to send the employees to attend an event outside the workplace. Once a speaker or instructor is on-site, you may have the opportunity to approach him or her directly for advice.

Create a Study Group

Create a study group within your department, team, or company to focus on a specific skill area. The group might meet once or twice a week to learn and practice new skills. You might choose to coordinate the study group but have different members or persons within or outside your group perform the actual instruction.

Submit Suggestions

Submit ideas to your company that can improve quality, save time, reduce expenses, and increase profit. Many companies have suggestion programs for this purpose. However, suggestions should be offered and welcomed whether or not a formal suggestion program is in place.

Publish a Paper or Newsletter

Write and publish a paper or newsletter that contributes to information exchange in your area of expertise or interest. The paper may be for internal company use or for an outside trade publication. Virtually everyone has acquired some knowledge or experience that someone else will find useful. If you believe you need some writing assistance, seek help from people within or outside your company who have the skills to constructively edit your material.

Serve As a Leader

Serve as leader to a team, task force, or project within your company. Serve as an officer in a professional society or for a professional event. Perform assignments that require you to take charge, make decisions, and work with others in using their collective knowledge and experiences toward accomplishing a common goal.

Present to a Group

Present to your department, team, organization, managers, customers, or professional society. You can begin with five-minute presentations and build up to more substantial speeches of half an hour or more. Presenting and teaching are effective ways to enhance your knowledge while helping others. You will inevitably learn from the questions, knowledge, and experiences of your audiences.

Improve a Process, Product, or Service

Search for ways to improve current processes, products, and services to make them more efficient or marketable. If you have an idea that has special merit, ask that you be allowed a window of work time to dedicate exclusively to development of the idea.

Take a Sabbatical

Work with your manager and company to arrange a sabbatical to study a specific subject area that will benefit you and your job. The length of sabbaticals vary, but they typically range from three months to one year. Many companies give wide latitude to managers to approve employee sabbaticals. You might even ask for a one-day sabbatical every so often to spend in the library, with customers, or "in the field" conducting research.

Seek Out a Mentor

Approach someone in your organization whose expertise you respect and ask if he or she will become your mentor. A mentor will help you effectively grow in the direction of your interests—usually a direction that has some correlation to the position or mission of the mentor. If there is no one inside your organization who you would like to mentor you, seek someone outside your company.

Initiate a Skill Enrichment Day

Propose and be willing to coordinate a half-day or full-day seminar aimed at improving the skill value of every employee in your organization. A Skill Enrichment Day will raise employees' awareness of the need to remain competitive in the skills they offer to the company. This event might even become an annual or semiannual activity.

Seek a Special Assignment

These positions, typically lasting anywhere from three months to two years, are primarily for employees who have demonstrated exceptional motivation and accomplishments. A special assignment position might offer an employee the opportunity to focus on a specific field of interest to them as well as to their company. The position of assistant to an executive allows an employee to develop skills by learning firsthand how veteran executives handle various issues.

Do you get the idea that the opportunities for skill enrichment are virtually limitless? Typically, those people who appear to contribute the most, to receive promotions and awards, and to obtain the most latitude to pursue their work are those who have made skill improvement a continuous and serious pursuit.

Develop and Execute Your Skill Enrichment Plan

When you have finished the exercise on page 162, examine the results and ask yourself the following questions:

- Did I finish the training events I started?
- Of the training events that I did not complete, were the reasons unavoidable or in my best long-term interests?
- Which training events offered a valuable application to my job?
- Which training events offered no value to my job?
- Am I satisfied with the overall progress that I have achieved?
- In retrospect, what would I have done differently?

The Skill Enrichment Plan

This plan helps you consciously improve your menu of skills so that your skill value not only continues to grow, but grows in the right direction. The Skill Enrichment Plan explores the actions you plan to take over the next twelve months to improve your skill value. The actual plan can be several sheets of paper with handwritten notes or a more formal typed document.

The Skill Enrichment Plan aims to accomplish the following:

1. **Describe your long-term skill objectives.**

   This part of the plan describes your major objective—the dream. The dream does not have to be grandiose; it need only be a goal that is meaningful enough for you to consciously and continuously pursue.

   One simple activity that you can pursue on an ongoing basis (whether or not you plan to seek a new job) is a periodical review of the classified ads in your local newspaper. Study the ads for the jobs similar to your present or desired occupation, and ask yourself if you have the skill value to be a strong applicant for these jobs. Keep in mind that the criteria to obtain a new position are often more stringent than those required to keep your present job.

2. **List the skills that you need to enhance or acquire.**

   A technique to identify these skills was presented earlier in this chapter. You should list all the skills you determined were necessary, whether or not you possess them at present. It is important to maintain a "big picture" perspective as you work on various aspects of your overall plan.

3. **Determine your skill objectives.**

   Next, identify the skills you would like to improve or acquire, and label them "skill objectives." Prioritize the list of skill objectives so that it is clear which skills must be developed before others. Then decide which of the higher priority skill needs can be addressed in the next twelve months (or sooner, if you prefer). If a specific skill requires years to master, ask yourself what you can do within a twelve-month period to make headway toward your overall objective. You might be pleasantly surprised at what you can achieve through several years of long-term planning.

4. **Identify the method you plan to use to achieve each skill objective.**

   This part of your plan describes *how* you plan to achieve each skill objective. You can select from the ideas presented earlier in this chapter, add your own, and use a combination of both. If specific people are needed to help you meet a given skill objective, identify these people in your plan. This stage of the Skill Enrichment Plan is especially enjoyable. If you take a few moments to visualize what your achievement can be at the end of the twelve months, you can feel a strong sense of accomplishment. This part of your plan also describes *when* you plan to achieve each of your skill objectives. It also addresses the impact that the execution of your plan will have on your work schedule and your personal time outside of work. Be sure to carefully balance the time you will commit to execution of your Skill Enrichment Plan with the time necessary to meet both your work-related and personal commitments.

   For example, if you are pursuing a college degree, but know travel or overtime will be required of you during an upcoming semester, plan a light school load during this period.

5. **Describe the benefit of each undertaking.**

   This part of your plan describes what's in it for you. This is a useful tool to help ensure that you appropriately prioritize your skill objectives and work only on those items that have valid short-term or long-term benefits. If you clearly understand the benefit of a given skill objective, you will likely give more of your time, energy, and passion to its pursuit.

Skill Enrichment Plan Guidelines

As you develop your Skill Enrichment Plan, here are a few guidelines to help in your planning:

1. **Don't intentionally overcommit.**

   If you put an overly ambitious plan into place, you may soon find yourself facing burnout. Make sure that your plan is achievable. A little stretching is good, but you don't want to break. If a year is too far to plan, then plan for every three to six months—whatever feels right to you. Revisit and reshape the plan whenever you feel it is necessary.

2. **Don't take on classes or training that you won't use.**

   Make wise use of your time. It is easy to get overly excited about classes and training and to enroll in everything that seems remotely interesting. When planning your training or education, stick with classes that are directly applicable to your short-term and long-term objectives.

3. **It's okay to change your mind.**

   If you are not sure what you want to do or be down the road, commit to some pursuit that you believe you will enjoy. If you later decide to change your mind, change it! However, if you find yourself constantly changing your mind and never actually following through on your commitments, there may be a deeper reason for your uncertainty.

4. **Seek out more help if necessary.**

   Although in most cases your manager will be the first person you consult to solicit help in developing your Skill Enrichment Plan, consider other resources your company may have to offer. Don't rule out guidance from outside your company—a university professor, a recognized authority in your field, or a professional counselor.

5. **Whenever possible, learn by doing.**

   People learn most effectively when they go beyond the classroom environment and learn through experience. Make sure that your Skill Enrichment Plan includes generous doses of "doing."

6. **Commit yourself to a lifetime of learning.**

   As Henry David Thoreau said, "In the long run, men only hit what they aim at." You are far more likely to attain your skill objectives if you keep a concentrated focus on them over the long term. Be prepared to make skill enrichment a lifetime undertaking.

▌▌▌ Exercise 13 ▌▌▌
Monitor Your Skill Enrichment

In the space provided, list all the activities related to skill enhancement that you have undertaken in the past twelve months. Include
items that resulted from on-the-job training that automatically
came your way. Next to each of the activities listed, indicate
whether or not you completed the activity. For example, if you
began a typing class, but quit the class before it was completed,
indicate this in the appropriate column.

Activity/Event	Completed?

▌ ▌ ▌

CHAPTER SIX

The Juggling Act:
Balancing Your Personal and Professional Lives

As we have come to see, the indispensable employee is not the person who works the longest hours, keeps quiet, and does the manager's bidding. Employees can optimize their value to the work force by actualizing their capacities in both their personal and professional lives. As we saw in Chapter 1, an employee brings to the workplace the relative satisfaction of his or her personal life. This chapter argues that it is necessary to find a balance between the two in order to maximize your value as an employee.

Are you enjoying your life? Is your life unfolding as you had planned or hoped? Are you managing your time and energies so that the endeavors most important to you are receiving the necessary attention? If you answer "yes" to all three questions, I applaud you. I believe you are among a small, fortunate segment of the population.

In the modern world, with all its complexities, people can put an excessive amount of time and energy into unfulfilling pursuits. This chapter aims to help you gain a new perspective on balancing your professional life with your personal life.

Understand the Value of Balance

The quality of the rest of your life depends on how you invest in it with your present actions. As you reflect on those things that seem important today, consider whether they will be important to you tomorrow. A year from now? Ten years from now? Thirty years from now? Are they even important enough today to warrant the priority you place on them?

You must decide what is important to you both for today and for years from now, then learn how to balance your

True or False?

Once again, all the statements below reflect common fallacies. As you read through them, ask yourself whether you have allowed any of the misconceptions to cloud your own perspective on the relationship between work and your personal life.

Personal contentment at home has little to do with your performance at work. ❏ True ❏ False

Comments:

Work satisfaction has little to do with your behavior at home. ❏ True ❏ False

Comments:

Success is defined by societal norms. ❏ True ❏ False

Comments:

It is not healthy to question your purpose in life, as there is no way to know the answer. ❏ True ❏ False

Comments:

True or False? (continued)

People with successful careers put
    work first, family second.
Comments:
                    ❑ True ❑ False

Spending some "quiet time" each day
    is an unproductive use of time.
Comments:
                    ❑ True ❑ False

Relaxation techniques work well at
    home but are not appropriate in
    the workplace setting.
Comments:
                    ❑ True ❑ False

There's no need to enroll in nutrition
    or exercise classes unless you're not
    feeling well.
Comments:
                    ❑ True ❑ False

You should wait until middle age to
    plan for your senior years.
Comments:
                    ❑ True ❑ False

actions to nurture both needs. In some cases, those things that seem important may not actually be meaningful in the long term. Further, some of what you judge to be unimportant today may become important to you down the road.

Life is all about balance. There are infinite choices to make, yet only a finite amount of time and resources to expend. You can focus your time and energy on one or many pursuits. Your return on investment will be directly proportionate to the concentration of your energy. Let's look at two simple examples.

Example #1: Matt aspires to become a corporate executive within the next ten years but is not willing to sacrifice any of his time or resources away from work to increase his skill value. Does this mean that he will not be able to achieve his career objectives? Not necessarily, but it does diminish his chances. Why? Because there are other people who *are* willing to sacrifice more of their personal life to realize their career aspirations. And the competition for the positions Matt aspires to is formidable, largely because of the personal investment that others are willing to make.

Example #2: Jennifer claims her family is the most important priority in her life, yet when faced with a decision, she almost always puts her family behind her career. She lives a very full and busy life, and endures a great deal of stress. It seems the strongest causes of her stress are the family situations that require her presence or intervention— children's school activities, time alone with her husband, family illnesses, and household chores.

Does the "pressure" from her family mean that Jennifer cannot find the desired time for work, friends, and hobbies?

BOJANGLES'

681 COBB PKWY NORTH
MARIETTA, GA 30062
888-300-4265
BOJANGLESATLANTA.COM

#0328   DT
1 L ICETEA   1.89

            SUBTOTAL   1.89
            TAX TOTL   .11
TOTAL   2.00
            XXXXXXXXXXXX3197
            VISA   2.00
Joseph   CSHR
1104 15:32 MAY 04'14   W/S#04 P1

Not necessarily. Does this mean her marriage and family life are doomed? Not necessarily. What it does mean, however, is that her weak investment in marriage and family matters is likely to show a low return on investment down the road. She may still have the marriage and family, but will it be everything she wants this "most important priority" in her life to be?

Are these examples meant to show how people make the wrong decisions in balancing their lives? Not at all. The examples are designed to illustrate that people have choices and that these choices should be made based on what is important in people's lives—both at present and years down the road. In the examples above, Matt and Jennifer *did* make choices, either knowingly or not, that were not aligned with the values they claimed as important. The point here is to be careful about the decisions you make by default. Once you decide what is important to you, make choices and decisions that support your priorities. Of course, there are more paths to pursue than the two extremes just mentioned. Hopefully, this chapter will help you find the path of balance.

> *You don't get to choose how you are going to die, or when.*
> *You can only decide how you are going to live.*
>
> Joan Baez

Recognize the Obstacles to Achieving Balance

It seems obvious that a balance between professional life and personal life offers many benefits. Why then is it so difficult to achieve? Let's examine a few prevalent reasons.

External Pressure

This may include the expectations of your spouse, boss, peers, parents, or spiritual, political, or social mentors. Because of the close personal association, it is natural to want to please these people. However, their influence can be very strong and there is often a tendency to put their wishes before one's own. While this principle may at best be selfless, be careful that you are not actually sacrificing your own personal and professional goals to please someone else.

Pursuit of Material Wealth

Everyone wants financial security; it is one of the main reasons that people work. Therefore, money will clearly factor into career and personal decisions, but be careful that you do not pursue material wealth to the exclusion of other important pursuits.

Disillusionment

Some people put in extra hours at work to escape an unhappy personal life. Others work less because they don't enjoy their job or job environment. In more extreme cases, people may become withdrawn in both their personal and professional lives due to depression or some other emotional trauma. Each of these situations erects an obstacle to achieving balance.

Inability to Say No

Although people who cannot confidently and comfortably say no to an added task or responsibility usually mean well, they undermine their own sense of personal balance. Everyone needs to learn when and how to tactfully say no.

Lack of a Clearly Defined Goal or Direction

It is essential that you set goals for yourself, or at least a general direction of pursuit.

Define Your Life Goals

The indispensable first step to getting the things you want out of life is this: decide what you want.

Ben Stein

Before you can satisfactorily balance your professional life with your personal life, you must know and understand your life goals—those pursuits that are most important to you in both the short and the long term. If you are uncertain of your life goals, then the major decisions you make will be subject more to outside influences than to your own best interests. In defining your life goals, keep in mind the following principles:

1. You can always change your goals. If you revisit your life plan periodically, you will almost certainly change your goals from time to time.

2. You don't have to go public. It is perfectly acceptable to keep your life goals to yourself.

3. Your life goals can help define a purpose for your life. If you do not already have a sense of purpose that is satisfactory to you, one will naturally evolve through the pursuit of these goals.

Now perform exercise 14. After completing the list, review the items for possible conflicts or duplications. Then prioritize the list (especially if the list has more than ten items) into "important" and "most important." You want to focus on the most important. The next step is to decide how you will proceed. What actions can you take and what choices can you make now and in the future to progress toward your goals? There are countless avenues, and you have the rest of your life to pursue them. Let's look at a few examples of choices people have made after completing this exercise:

- One woman decided to take advantage of the training and job opportunities available in her company so she could eventually move into a job that is more aligned with her interests and talents.

- A man chose to forgo buying a new car every two years. Instead, he will buy one every four years and set aside at least half of the money he saves to build his dream home when he retires.

- An executive realized he was sacrificing too much time with his family in order to pursue his career. One of his immediate actions was to set aside one or more full days each month exclusively for family time.

Take Actions to Improve the Balance

This section offers advice for balancing a healthy personal life with a productive work life. While most of the ideas presented here are fairly universal, there are countless other measures you can take that will be unique to your own situation.

▮ ▮ ▮ Exercise 14 ▮ ▮ ▮
Life Goals

In the space provided, list the goals that are or will be important to you over the course of your life. Try to list each item on a single line; if your list becomes too long to fit in the space provided, continue on a separate piece of paper. Try to be uninhibited with your idea generation, but stick to the goals—lofty or not, spiritual or material—that are genuinely important to you. In other words, if you would *like* to win a Pulitzer Prize, but it is not truly important to you, don't list it. Ask yourself the following question: If I were writing my own obituary, what would I judge to be the most important experiences or endeavors of my life?

Example:

1. Be financially secure, particularly during my senior years.

2. Maintain optimal health.

3. Master a profession or skill of my choice.

1. _____

2. _____

3. _____

4. _____

5. _____

6. _____

7. _____

▮ ▮ ▮

Set Aside Time for "Nonwork"

Sometimes the concerns people bring with them to the workplace keep them from focusing their full attention on the tasks at hand. Set aside time in your day to concentrate on these matters rather than allow them to infringe on the mental and emotional energy required by your work throughout the day.

Plan Your Finances

Chances are good that some of the life goals you listed in the previous exercise require money. You can plan your finances on your own with the help of books or classes, or you can seek help from an accountant or financial advisor. The time you invest now to understand and plan your financial future can save you time, money, and frustration in the future.

Plan Holidays and Vacations With Family and Friends

If you would like to spend more quality time with your mate, your children, or your friends then set aside holidays and vacation days for that purpose. Of course, weekends and evenings throughout the week can also be made available for home-based "vacations."

Exercise Regularly

If one or more of your life goals mentions health (or requires that you be around for at least several more years), plan an exercise regimen to keep you fit. Exercise benefits not only physical health, but quality of life as well.

Improve Your Productivity

Look for ways to improve your productivity in the tasks you routinely perform both at work, at home, and in your recreation. Increased productivity offers not only intrinsic satisfaction, but also helps to free time for other duties and interests.

Maintain a Lighthearted Attitude

Remember how uninhibited you were as a young child? How easily you laughed? How you approached everything with playful wonder? You may find it very refreshing to bring back some of that lightheartedness into your adult life. Try to laugh more; let yourself be entertained by the vast diversity of experience life offers.

Work at Home

If you are able to, consider working at home more often. This will provide a change of environment that can boost productivity, reduce stress, and allow you more time with your loved ones.

Cultivate a Hobby

You can develop a skill that will enhance your current career, help you in your next one, or keep you active in your retirement years. A hobby by definition should be a relaxing, fulfilling undertaking for you, not an endeavor that will add stress to your life.

Seek Out Additional Education

Seek out education in areas that will help you achieve your life goals. This education may involve earning a high school equivalency certificate, seeking a master's degree, or acquiring specialized training.

Simplify Your Life

Learn to appreciate and focus on what you have, rather than dwell on what you don't have. Discard any emotional or material "baggage" that unnecessarily complicates your life. When your mind is too heavily laden with thoughts and intentions, you can't focus clearly and intensely on the pursuit of those things that are important to you.

Introduce Variety Into Your Life

Break out of your routines and patterns from time to time. Get out of bed an hour earlier than usual and take a walk around the block. Drive a new route home from work. Unplug the television for one week. Subscribe to an out-of-town newspaper. See a movie in the middle of the day. Rent your dream car. Breaking out of the routine can give you a sense of release and freedom that will in turn renew your enthusiasm.

Take a Mental Health Day

A mental health day is a day away from work, chores, and all obligations. You can do whatever you want or nothing at all. What's important is to allow your mind and psyche to take a rest from their usual pressures.

Live a Healthier Lifestyle

Enroll in courses that educate you about healthy lifestyle alternatives. These courses can address anything from low-fat cooking to smoking cessation to fitness training.

Learn and Practice Relaxation Techniques

Relaxation techniques cover a wide spectrum of activities—breathing exercises, meditation, visualization, and massage to name a few. Find a technique that works for you and include it in your daily routine. Many relaxation techniques can be practiced anywhere—in the office, on an airplane—and all can be practiced at home. Most will require at least a few minutes of solitude and ideally some peace and quiet. Continue with your preferred technique until your heart rate slows, your breathing is even, and your mind is quiet. This is a great way to prevent stress, clear your head, and soothe your nerves.

Develop a Life Goals Plan

You have now listed your life goals and have been introduced to some actions you can take to achieve them. This section will show you how to better define what each life goal means to you and to develop a plan to ensure that each goal is attained. Whether your plan is neatly typed or scribbled on paper, the act of writing down the plan will strengthen your commitment to it. This process helps you to better realize what is needed to achieve your life goals and reinforces that *you* are the one who will bring them to fruition. Let's examine the steps in developing your Life Goals Plan.

1. **List your life goals.**

   This part you've already done.

2. **Qualify what each goal means.**

   Try to define the goal in tangible, measurable terms. Visualize the end result of each goal and how you will feel when the goal is reached.

3. **Identify how each goal can be attained.**

   For each life goal, list the actions you must take to ensure that the goal will be reached. Visualize how you will feel upon completion of each action.

4. **Where applicable, assign target dates to each action.**

   Identify approximate dates when each action should be completed. It is okay to list the month, quarter of the year, or even year for some actions—a precise date is not necessary.

5. **Repeat Steps 1-4 every six months.**

   Reexamine your Life Goals Plan every six months or so. Reflect on the progress you have made and update each step as needed. Don't forget to first update your full list of life goals; that is, add, delete, or revise the goals in accordance with any changes in your plans, thoughts, or desires.

As you can see, creating your Life Goals Plan is simple. However, the application of these steps can require a lot of effort. But, as discussed earlier, the benefit you gain will be directly proportionate to the effort you invest.

Earlier in this chapter, a sample list of life goals was identified. Let's use the three entries to illustrate each of the

Life Goals Plan steps just described. Assume the person in the example just turned 35 years old in January of this year.

Step 1. List Life Goals

- Be financially secure most of my life, but particularly during my senior years.
- Maintain optimal health.
- Master a profession or skill of my choice.

Step 2. Qualify Each Life Goal

Financial. To have assets worth $200,000 by the time I reach the age of 45, and $500,000 by the time I reach the age of 65.

Health. To be within ten pounds of my preferred body weight beginning at age 36. To be within the recommended healthy cholesterol range beginning at age 37. To begin a routine exercise program that will contribute to a blood pressure range of 100 to 120 (systolic) and 60 to 70 (diastolic) and a standing heartbeat rate of 55 to 65 beats per minute—all within six months of turning 36. To understand what a good nutritional diet is and to consume fresh vegetables and fruits as at least 50 percent of my diet each day by the age of 36. To be able to relax within two minutes of beginning a relaxation technique within six months of turning 36.

Mastery of a skill. To have identified, by age 36, a skill that I would like to master. To have attained a recognized mastery of that skill by the time I am 45 years old.

Steps 3 & 4. List Actions–and Target dates–to Attain Each Goal

Financial. Consult a certified financial advisor to help lay out a workable plan–which includes identifying educational offerings for me to pursue. To be accomplished by March of this year.

Health. Consult a certified nutritionist to help lay out a workable plan–which includes identifying educational offerings for me to pursue. To be accomplished by June of this year. Consult a certified physical therapist to help lay out a workable plan—which includes identifying educational offerings for me to pursue. To be accomplished by September of this year. Consult a certified "stress-reduction" therapist to help lay out a workable plan–which includes identifying education offerings for me to pursue. To be accomplished by January of next year.

Mastery of a skill. Using the resources of my manager and company, develop a Skill Enrichment Plan that puts me on track to mastery of the desired skill by the time I reach age 45. To be accomplished by April of next year.

Let's take a closer look at this example. In Step 2, the goals were qualified in further detail, and a time limit was set for the implementation of each step. It is important to define what these goals actually mean to you, as a term such as "financially secure" opens itself to a wide scope of definitions. Steps 3 and 4 were combined in the example, but ideally Step 3 should be completed before Step 4. Notice that the "mastery of a skill" entry assumed the person in the example worked for a company that either offered jobs related to the desired skills or had the resources to help implement the Skill Enrichment Plan. In actuality, many people may need to seek help outside their company. Also notice that the target dates to complete the actions have been scattered to allow a reasonable amount of time before beginning each action. It is okay to set ambitious target dates, but make sure they are also reasonable enough to fit your schedule and routine. After working with a consultant, the person in the example will probably have a list of numerous actions to replace the single act of "working with a consultant."

The following section offers additional thoughts that you may find helpful as you strive to bring balance into your life.

But I Can't Find the Time!

Everyone needs and deserves to take time for themselves, but people are quick to list the reasons why they can't find the time. You *can* find time if you make it a high priority in your life. I recently heard the following story of one woman who found a creative solution to this problem.

Wendy desperately needed some quiet time to herself. She has a husband, three children, and demanding sixteen-hour days, seven days a week. There seemed never to be an end to her duties as wife, mother, homemaker, errand person, schoolwork tutor, activities planner, and more. The family had decided to take a three-day weekend vacation at a cabin near a beach so that everyone could relax and have some fun.

Wendy, anticipating that she would do most of the work, said she would participate in the weekend only on the condition that she alone would start the vacation two days early. During the two days, she would shop for groceries and get the cabin ready for the weekend. But she needed some time to herself. The family agreed. During the two days, Wendy was able to lie on the beach and read a book she had been unable to enjoy. When the rest of the family arrived, she was rested and ready to enjoy their company.

What happened? A win-win for everyone. The quiet time gave Wendy a chance for a much needed break from routine. And, of course, the rest of the family appreciated the stocked cupboards and refrigerator. The mini-vacation turned out to be a great vacation for everyone.

Set Aside Family Time

One of the most common regrets of fathers, and increasingly of mothers, is that they wish they had found more time to be with their children when the children were young and at home. Do you know your children's best friends? Their favorite sports or school subjects? Their favorite movies, toys, and memories?

Find ways to include your spouse or children in your day-to-day activities, or include yourself in theirs. When you run an errand, take one or more of your children along. Occasionally have lunch with them during the summer or go out to dinner throughout the year. Invite your children, one at a time, to share a day with you at your workplace. Take one of your children on a business trip. Yes, a business trip. Where there is a will, there is always a way.

Make Good Use of Your Time

Many times I have heard people say they sleep late whenever they can, not because they are tired, but because they don't know what else they would do with their time. And how many times have you heard someone say, "Do you want to...?" and heard the ready response of "Sure! I don't have anything better to do"? Sometimes people have the time but not a goal or purpose to pursue. Perhaps the greatest waste of all is the waste of time. Once it has passed, it can never be recovered. Knowing your life goals and using this information to create a plan can add greatly to the enjoyment and fulfillment you derive from each day that passes.

As people age, they become increasingly aware of the clock ticking away. They find themselves working harder and more deliberately at making better choices that will impact the future.

For virtually everyone, life unfolds according to the actions they take. These actions will directly or indirectly influence the future. It is not too late to learn how to make the best use of your time today so that you can both enjoy the present and invest in the future.

Ask yourself the following questions:

▊ Do I really understand my life goals?
▊ Are my current life goals what I truly want?
▊ Am I taking these goals into account as I make choices to balance my life in favor of the things that are the most important to me?

It is essential that you take the time to ask these questions, answer them as candidly and as thoughtfully as you can, and drive your actions in a direction that allows you to answer yes to each of them in the future. Take time to know yourself, know what is important to you, and enjoy your life journey.

Appendix

Exercises

The exercises in this book are meant to assist you in various aspects of your personal and professional growth. Because this growth is an ongoing activity, you are encouraged to regularly revisit the exercises. The publisher grants the reader permission to reproduce the exercises in this appendix for his or her own use.

▎ ▎ ▎ Exercise 1 ▎ ▎ ▎
Stepping Stones

In the space provided, list at least ten things that you can do today that you frequently "failed at" in the process of learning. List anything that comes to mind, whether it happened yesterday or when you were a child. Here are a few examples; riding a bike, skating, typing, driving a car, using chopsticks, playing a musical instrument. Try to include unique skills or characteristics that you have developed over the years in your jobs, hobbies, relationships, etc. Examples of these might include patience, listening skills, public speaking, etc.

When you feel the list is sufficiently complete, consciously recall any pain, embarrassment, or frustration you encountered as you were developing these skills. Also bring to mind those moments of breakthrough you experienced along the way, and remember the sense of pride and accomplishment you felt.

1. _____

2. _____

3. _____

4. _____

5. _____

6. _____

7. _____

8. _____

9. _____

10. _____

■ ■ ■

Constructive and Destructive Criticism

Below try to develop a list of at least five criticisms that you have received in the last few days including those that took place on the telephone or through correspondence. List every remark, no matter how seemingly insignificant. Examine each item and decide whether it is an example of constructive (C) or destructive (D) criticism. If you can learn anything at all of value, mark it as constructive. As you mark each entry, recall how you felt when you received the criticism. Recall the incident and visualize yourself handling the criticism with poise. Then extract any valuable learning offered by the criticism. Repeat for each item in the list.

Examples:

Criticism	Constructive (C)	Destructive (D)
1. Ann said my meeting minutes were late.	✔	
2. Dennis said my memo was too wordy.	✔	
3. Norm gave me a disapproving look when I did not side with him on this issue.		✔

▪ ▪ ▪

Constructive and Destructive Criticism (continued)

Criticism	Constructive (C)	Destructive (D)
1.		
2.		
3.		
4.		
5.		

▌ ▌ ▌

| ▌ ▌ **Exercise 3** ▌ ▌ |
Determine Your Risk-Taking Style

To understand your risk-taking style, list below several of the risks you have taken in the past year. Include both small and large risks, and state each risk in just a few words. When you have completed your list of at least five risks, assign each action one of the following letters in the column provided: S (small risk), M (medium risk), or L (large risk). Is your level of risk taking what you thought it would be? Ask yourself if you are satisfied with the risks you have undertaken in the past year. If no, why not?

Whether you are satisfied or not, you might find it helpful to go on to the second list, which allows you to identify the risks you would like to pursue in the next six to twelve months. Again identify each risk as S, M, or L. In the last column, identify a specific time or opportunity to carry out the risk. You might, for example, identify one risk that you will pursue each week or month, and another risk that will be taken at tomorrow's staff meeting.

Past Risks	(S)	(M)	(L)
1.			
2.			
3.			
4.			
5.			

▌ ▌ ▌

Future Risks	(S)	(M)	(L)	When
1.				
2.				
3.				
4.				
5.				

| | |

▌ ▌ ▌ Exercise 4 ▌ ▌ ▌
Pros and Cons

This exercise describes a technique to help you make a difficult decision. Take a few moments to ponder a decision confronting you. In the space provided, describe the decision in the form of a question. The question should be worded such that it can be answered with either a "yes" or a "no." Now, take either position in answering the question. In the column marked "Pros," write the advantages of this course of action, and in the column marked "Cons," express the disadvantages.

In order to weigh the pros and cons, assign each a value of 3 (high), 2 (medium), or 1 (low), then tabulate the total for each column. If one column has a significantly higher score than the other, your decision should be relatively easy—the higher score prevails. However, if the scores are close, then more thought is required before you make the final decision. In this case, focus mostly on the items to which you assigned a value of three.

Note: If you believe it will be helpful, solicit information from friends, family, and coworkers to help you develop the list of pros and cons. The information you gather may help you see more objectively and realistically the perceived advantages and disadvantages of your decision. The information can also help you test the outcome of making the decision—before it has been made. But remember, the ultimate responsibility for making the decision rests with you; be careful not to empower other people to make decisions *for* you.

▌ ▌ ▌

▎ ▌ ▊ Exercise 4 ▊ ▌ ▎
Pros and Cons (continued)

Decision:			
Pros	1, 2, or 3	Cons	1, 2, or 3
1.			
2.			
3.			
4.			
5.			
Total Value of Pros: _____		Total Value of Cons: _____	

▊ ▊ ▊

▎ ▎ ▉ Exercise 5 ▉ ▎ ▎
Keep Your Eye on the Goal

In the space below, identify a goal—small or large—that you have avoided pursuing for some time. Perhaps one or more of the inhibitive behaviors listed previously has prevented you from moving forward, or perhaps you have procrastinated for some other reason. It doesn't matter. List at least five reasons why it is important to you to attain this goal. After you have contemplated the reasons, rank them from 1 to 5 in order of their meaningfulness to you and your life. These are the primary catalysts that will help energize you when your perseverance begins to weaken.

Goal:	
Catalysts:	Rank (1-5)
1.	
2.	
3.	
4.	
5.	

▉ ▉ ▉

▌▌▌ Exercise 6 ▌▌▌
Obstacles to Happiness

In the space provided, list several things that you believe detract from or limit your happiness. Be totally honest with yourself. You can list people, events, situations, or anything else, but try to be specific. Write "My colleague constantly complains about my work" rather than "my colleague."

When the list is complete, examine each entry carefully and plot it on the matrix according to whether the obstacle is controllable or uncontrollable, and whether it represents an internal belief or an external situation. Consider these three examples:

1. I don't deserve to be happy (C, I)
2. I am consistently passed over for promotions (C, E)
3. I am losing my hair (U, E)

Items in quadrants 1 and 2 represent situations that you can change. Example 1 is an internal belief that can be (and should be) reversed. Example 2 can also be reversed. The person should investigate the reasons that he or she is consistently passed over for promotions, and take measures to address them. Example 3 represents an uncontrollable, external situation. As such, it cannot be reversed. It is futile to worry about items in quadrant 3; your energies are best spent accepting the situation and learning how to live with it. If you have plotted anything in quadrant 4, think again. There are *no* internal feelings or beliefs that you do not have the power to control.

▌ ▌ ▌

▮ ▮ ▮ Exercise 6 ▮ ▮ ▮
Obstacles to Happiness (continued)

	Controllable	Uncontrollable
Internal	1.	4.
External	2.	3.

▮ ▮ ▮

▎❙❚ Exercise 7 ▎❙❚
Empowerment and Solutions

In the space provided, list the problems currently confronting you—problems that inhibit the progress of your job. Then examine each entry and decide if the problem is really yours—not someone else's—and, if so, how you might resolve it. Keep the notion of empowerment in mind as you brainstorm possible solutions for each situation. For now, be as creative as possible with your ideas; you can go back later and decide the feasibility and appropriateness of each potential solution.

Problem	Possible Solutions
1.	
2.	
3.	
4.	
5.	

❚ ❚ ❚

❙ ❚ ❚ Exercise 8 ❚ ❚ ❙
Control Your Commitments

In the space provided, list all the commitments you have made that are still outstanding. It doesn't matter if they are ongoing or are already overdue. In the columns next to each entry, indicate the date you made the commitment and the date you plan to fulfill the commitment. Now look at the list and decide for yourself if your commitments are under control, that is, are they achievable and within reason?

Commitment	Date Made	Date to Be Fulfilled

❚ ❚ ❚

Problem-Solving Options

In the space provided, list the problems that you have complained about over the past several days. Then examine the list for the entries that actually resulted in some valuable change being made. Next, for each entry, ask yourself if it is worth your time and your manager's time to have you work at solving the problem.

Problem or Complaint	Did It Change?	Is It Worth It?

█ █ █

▮ ▮ ▮ Exercise 10 ▮ ▮ ▮
Skillful Communication

Recall three or four instances in which you said something you later wished you hadn't. Briefly describe each incident in the space provided below. Now examine the use of speech guidelines in the previous section and note any that apply to the regrettable situations. How could observation of one or more of the guidelines have prevented you from saying something you later regretted?

Incident	Relevant Guidelines	Rank

Next, go through the ten guidelines and rank them in order of their relevance to your own personal and professional growth. In other words, the comment marked "1" should be the guideline you believe you most need to improve in practice. Make an effort to honor the guidelines at work, home, and wherever else you go. Especially keep in mind the suggestions you ranked highly.

This simple exercise can considerably raise your awareness of the impact your words have on other people. Even a careful study of these guidelines is, of course, no guarantee that you won't again say something you later regret, but a review of the list from time to time will help you remain aware of verbal minefields.

▮ ▮ ▮

▎ ▎ ▊ Exercise 11 ▊ ▎ ▎
Define Your Customer

In the space below, list all the people within your organization to whom you provide a product or service. In the second column, describe what you offer to them, and in the third mark how often you provide the product or service.

Customer	Product/Service	How Often?
1.		
2.		
3.		
4.		
5.		
6.		
7.		
8.		
9.		
10.		

▊ ▊ ▊

▌▐ █ Exercise 12 █ ▌▐
Whose customer are you?

In the space provided, list all the people, departments, and organizations of which you are a customer. In the second column, list what products or service they provide, and in the third column, evaluate the service you receive from them on a scale of one to ten. You can make notes next to the rating to support your evaluation.

Supplier	Product/Service	Rating	Comments
1.			
2.			
3.			
4.			
5.			
6.			
7.			
8.			
9.			
10.			

█ █ █

Monitor Your Skill Enrichment

In the space provided, list all the activities related to skill enhancement that you have undertaken in the past twelve months. Include items that resulted from on-the-job training that automatically came your way. Next to each of the activities listed, indicate whether or not you completed the activity. For example, if you began a typing class, but quit the class before it was completed, indicate this in the appropriate column.

Activity/Event	Completed?

▌ ▌ ▌

▌ ▌ ▌ Exercise 14 ▌ ▌ ▌
Life Goals

In the space provided, list the goals that are or will be important to you over the course of your life. Try to list each item on a single line; if your list becomes too long to fit in the space provided, continue on a separate piece of paper. Try to be uninhibited with your idea generation, but stick to the goals—lofty or not, spiritual or material—that are genuinely important to you. In other words, if you would *like* to win a Pulitzer Prize, but it is not truly important to you, don't list it. Ask yourself the following question: If I were writing my own obituary, what would I judge to be the most important experiences or endeavors of my life?

Example:

1. Be financially secure, particularly during my senior years.
2. Maintain optimal health.
3. Master a profession or skill of my choice.

1. _____

2. _____

3. _____

4. _____

5. _____

6. _____

7. _____

▌ ▌ ▌

INDEX

A

Accomplishment. *See* Achievement

Accomplishments, memory of, 10

Accountablility, on the job, 51

Achievement
 affirmation for, 45
 Henry Ford on, 30
 and perseverance, 28

Apathy, in problem solving, 80

Appearance, with customers, 132-133

Appreciation. *See* Praise

Aristotle, 10

Assistance, 103-105, 133

Assumptions, vs. questions, 116,118

Athletes, and instinct, 88

Attitude, 106-109
 in customer service, 132
 lighthearted, 175
 and productivity, 150
 and success or failure, 107

B

Bad news, disclosing, 114

Baez, Joan, 169

Baggage, emotional, 176

Balance, 165-177
 actions to improve, 172, 173-177
 recognizing obstacles, 169-171

Baseline, in continuous improvement. 84

Biases, overcoming, 43-44

Big picture perspective, 158

C

Carnegie, Dale, 20, 33

Closure, in problem solving, 79-80

Commitments
    in customer service, 134
    exercise, 75
    making blindly,76-77
    meeting, 70, 72-77
    and risk, 76
    and time management, 61

Communication. *See also* Bad News; Listening; Questions
    conflict in, 95
    exercise, 115
    guidelines, 110-111
    when meeting people, 109-110
    People Principles, 118-119
    respect in, 95-96
    words, 110

Complacency, and risk avoidance, 19

Complaining, about problems, 77-78

Concentration. *See* Focus

Conflict, in interpersonal communication, 95

Constructive criticism, 11-13
    exercise, 16-17

Contingency plan, and commitments, 74, 76

Continuous improvement, 83-87
    and problems, 113
    of skills, 140, 141-142

Control
    giving to others, 13
    of your life, 24-25

Conventional thinking, challenging, 89-90

Coolidge, Calvin, 25

Crane, George, 52

Criticism, 10-17
    giving in private, 101

Customer. *See also* Customer service
    defining your (*exercise*), 127
    interviewing, 126, 129-132
    you as a, 123, 126, 128 (*exercise*)
Customer service, 123-135. *See also* Customer internal and
    external, 123
    proposing changes in, 130-131
    Ten rules of contact, 132-135

D

Deadlines. *See* Commitments
Decision making, 24-25
    exercise, 26-27
    as risk avoidance, 19
Defects and customer service, 134
    eliminating, 87
Destructive criticism, 12-14,
    exercise, 16-17
Discarding, of unnecessary material, 65
Discipline. *See* Time management
Disillusionment, 170
Dissenter, in an escalation, 80
Diversity, in the workplace, 109
Door, closing your, 66
Dream job, planning for, 146
Dyer, Wayne W., 33, 39

E

Electronic bulletin board, 153
Emotional scars, from criticism, 15
Employment, earning every day, 52
Empowerment, 67-70
    exercise, 71

revising, 60
and risk, 20
short-term, 32
Ben Stein on, 171
Thoreau on, 161
setting, 52-53, 57-60
Golden Rule, 95
Guilt, 4, 37-39

H

Happiness, 33-34, 38-42
Health, 174, 176-177. *See also* Life Goals Plan
Help, 103-105, 133
Herodotus, 20
Hobby, cultivating a, 175
Home, working at, 175
Humor, 108-109

I

Initiative, taking the, 57-58
Improvement. *See* Continuous improvement; Innovation
Innovation, 90-91, 155
Interpersonal communication. *See* Communication
Insecurity. *See* Fear; Self-Esteem
Instincts, 87-88
Internal customer, defined, 123
Issue, vs. problem, 80

J
Job, 52
dream job, 146

Job dissatisfaction, 52
Job loss, 52
    and skills, 141
    sudden, 144-145
Job security
    not guaranteed, 139
    and skill enhancement, 146

L

Leader, serving as a, 155.
    See also Manager
Learning
    additional education, 176
    and the brain, 145
    influences on, 95
    and questions, 117
    by teaching, 105-106
Life Goals Plan, 177-181
Listening, 96-97
Lists, To-Do, 61-63
Loyalty, 141
Luck, 144

M

Mail, reviewing, 65-66
Management, role in escalations, 80, 82
Manager
    and customers, 134
    and empowerment, 67-68
    making a hero, 111-112
    and skill enhancement, 145-147, 149, 152
    and your goals, 57-58
Meditation, 177
Mental Health Day, 176

Self-Doubting behavior, 4

Self-Esteem, 3, 4, 13, 44, 45

Self-Expectations, and success and failure, 42-44

Self-Reliance, need for, 57-58

Service. *See* Customer service

Setbacks, recovering from, 91-92

Shakespeare, 44

Skills, 139-162
> development, 140-141, 144-146
> defining your needs, 146-151
> skill enrichment, 151-161
> *exercise*, 162

Solution-Oriented attitude, 77-78

Solutions, in problem solving, 78-79

Speakers, inviting, 153-154

Stein, Ben, 171

Stress. *See* Health; Relaxation

Study group, 154

Success. *See also* Failure
> Henry Ford on, 42
> and skill enhancement, 157
> Thoreau on, 47

Suggestions, submitting, 154

Surprises, 113-114

T

Talents, discovering, 5, 19-20

Targets, setting achievable, 86

Team membership
> and personal beliefs, 88-89
> and communication, 105

Telephone calls, returning, 66

Thoreau, Henry David, 47, 161